Speak, Memory: *Bookmarked*

Vladimir Nabokov's
Speak, Memory

BOOKMARKED

SVEN BIRKERTS

PUBLISHING

New York, NY

Printed in the United States of America
10 9 8 7 6 5 4 3 2 1

Ig Publishing
Box 2547
New York, NY 10163

www.igpub.com

ISBN: 978-1-63246-107-0

For my family—Lynn, Mara, and Liam—and for my mother, Sylvia, who keeps the sense of the long-ago world fresh for me.

In reality, every reader, while he reads, is the reader of himself. The writer's work is only a kind of optical instrument which he offers to the reader so that he might make out what, without this book, he might perhaps not have seen in himself.

—Proust

Note

WHEN I FINALLY DECIDED THAT *Speak, Memory* would be the book I would write about in a personal and also reflective way, I had to settle on what felt like the right approach. I have been an admirer of Vladimir Nabokov since I first came upon *Lolita* in my early twenties. And though I came to the memoir a few years later, I had by then read a number of his novels, along with his various lectures on literature. And my head was full of Nabokov lore: from interviews, critical essays, and incidentals from the literary gossip mill. But this was to be a short book, not a study, and I feared I would lose myself in tangents if I tried to say everything I wanted to about the man.

My best bet, I thought, was to write just about *Speak, Memory.* I would, as much as possible, approach it as an isolated text—even though I knew I would not be able to avoid occasional outside references, either to what I knew of the life, or else to my reading of other works. I would not read any background on the memoir, and would not make use of what insightful things others have said.

Once I had set my constraints, I held to them. I did not wander far afield, and I have very rarely quoted any one else on anything. But when I had finished, said what I had wanted to say, I could not resist checking in with other sources, especially Brian Boyd's deeply researched and detailed two-volume biography. It was in Boyd that I found the memoirist contradicted in certain telling ways. And while my approach did not allow me to go back to mix my reading with extraneous findings, these "posthumous" insights could not be ignored altogether. They shed interesting—and important—light on the memoirist's psychology and were very relevant to many things I had been exploring.

I have therefore added a few of these "other" insights as a kind of appendix. While they don't significantly change my assessment, they do invite the reader to elasticize her views on Nabokov's presentation, his fidelity to what really happened. The upshot, not surprisingly, is that he was a writer who favored the spirit of the law over its letter.

Prologue

I WAS HAVING LUNCH LAST summer in a seafood restaurant in Newport, Rhode Island when I unexpectedly got the itch. I had just taken part in a panel discussion about literary magazines and editing, and my co-panelists and I were eating oysters and calamari and making post-talk small talk about our projects. At one point, the woman who was hosting us mentioned that she was at work on a book-length-project about a book that had been influential in her life. There was a publisher, she said, dedicated to select one-book explorations that combined the personal and the literary.

I don't perk up easily, but now I did. Reading books has been the main through-line in my life. I spent many years as a bookseller and book dealer before I tried my hand at reviewing. After some years of that, I started writing longer and more reflective essays on authors and books. Then, still more years later, I published a short book called *Reading Life: Books for the Ages*, in which each essay recounted my reading experience with a different novel. I had so many favorites to choose from. I ended writing about just a few, like *The Moviegoer, To the Lighthouse, The Ambassadors*, and *Lolita*. Each novel had marked my life in some special way. I very much enjoyed approaching these novels from a more personal angle, but I also realized that the essay form was just not roomy enough. I ended each reflection with the feeling that there was so much more to be said.

Hearing about this series naturally excited me. I began scheming as soon as I started my drive back to Boston. And when I got home, I looked up the publisher right away and wrote to ask if they were still accepting pitches. I had my reply a few hours later: what book did I want to propose?

Now, after all this eager haste, I had to pause and give the matter some serious thought. There are, like I said, a number of books that I feel have been decisive in my life—books that reshaped my outlook and sometimes even affected my course of action. At seventeen, as suggestible as a college freshman can be, I read Henry Miller's *Tropic of Cancer* and spent months planning how I would expatriate myself to Europe. D.H. Lawrence's *Women in Love* all but defined my romantic outlook in high school. Julio Cortazar's *Hopscotch* fired my early writing ambitions . . . How would I decide?

Thinking in terms of a proposal, I turned the beam of my attention this way and that, trying to imagine what book I would be interested in writing about in that personal/literary way, and at some length. *Memoirs of Hadrian, The Alexandria Quartet, To the Lighthouse* . . . ? My list got longer the more I contemplated.

Unable to decide, I thought to work from the other direction. Instead of thinking about one book or another, I would concentrate on my inclinations and preoccupations, trying to isolate what basic themes I am now most compelled by in my own life. The book I chose would have to offer me the best pretext for delving there. When I put the question that way, the answer came almost immediately: Vladimir Nabokov's *Speak, Memory*. I had no second thoughts, and I knew why. Nabokov, more than any writer I'd read—even more than Proust, I'd say—was obsessively occupied with time, with memory, and with the search for meaningful patterns in his life.

Time, memory, patterns—my choice was not surprising. These are my own themes, too. The older I get the more these questions come alive in my thoughts. They have long since moved from conjecture to immediacy. And though reading is often considered to be a passive activity, real engagement with a book is anything but. Here, with the choice of Nabokov, what had started as an itch looked to become something much more serious, something more like what Walker Percy called a "search," an inner project of some urgency.

And then—it almost goes without saying—there was the dark delight of Nabokov's prose. Language used with such inventive accuracy is its own consideration, even as it creates and carries the content. I'm a sucker for a masterful style, never mind that, as Nabokov observed on the very first page of *Lolita*, "You can always count on a murderer for a fancy prose style." His way of saying this sounds almost flip, but the more I immerse myself in his writing, the more I find myself picking up that vibration, some of the coldness and calculation that we associate with a murderer. This, too, is part of the layering that provokes me.

The real Nabokov influence, *Speak, Memory*, actually came late. I was already married and we had a child. I'd kept the memoir on my shelves forever, one of many souvenirs from my years of dealing books. I'd been living in Ann Arbor—which in the 1970s was a true book town—when I first contracted my mania. It took me over. I would make my way to every book sale I could find, buying up books to re-sell, or else add to the library I fancied I was building. This was when I began my decade-long career as a bookseller and—briefly—dealer. Prizes were everywhere in those days. One of my many finds was a clean hardcover copy of *Speak, Memory*. I didn't know much, but and I knew enough to know that this was a book I should own. I gave it a place on the shelf with all the other books I promised myself I would one day get to. It was in one of the book boxes I sent to Boston when I finally moved, and when I reassembled my library it once again found its place on my 'to read' shelf.

The question can be asked: do we find certain books, or do they find us? No one knows, of course, but the idea that there might be a right book at the right time remains interesting to contemplate. If at all true, it's a rare event. I have hardly ever started a book and discovered as I read that it was the very thing I needed. For that reason, it feels like great luck when it happens out of the blue. But when it does, I usually find that some subliminal thread of awareness already exists. Having spent a good part of my adult life with books—reading them, browsing them, selling them, and spending whole workdays reading blurbs and book-jackets as I shelved, talking with customers, and sampling whatever looked interesting, I have acquired a cloudy half-knowing about many things. It's a mainly superficial acquisition, but one that can come in handy at pretentious dinner parties—it is, of course, of no use at all when talking to a scholar.

After years of this book life, I was full of inklings about writers and their works. Now that I had a better sense of the literary terrain, it happened more often that a certain mood would lead me toward some particular book. I would sense that there was something I needed. And so often there was. I have since come to trust this instinct.

With Nabokov, it was somehow different. I had read and enjoyed a few of his novels in college—they were there on the shelf, right alongside *Speak, Memory*. I had, I should say, looked at the memoir once or twice, but for some reason had always put it back. It didn't seem to have much plot; it seemed, at a glance, rooted in all sorts of historical specifics. I let it stay just within arm's reach, waiting for me. And then one day something happened. I can't remember the circumstance, but I was triggered—and I took it down for a closer look.

The synapses sparked as soon as I opened to the first page and read: "The cradle rocks above an abyss, and common sense tells us that our existence is but a brief crack of light between two eternities of darkness." That itself was like a sudden burst of illumination. I started right in and never looked back—I was caught up and I stayed caught up. The lyricism, the unwinding brilliance of the sentences, the atmospheres, the coloration of its many nostalgias . . . I find it hard to do justice to the feeling of that first reading. It was one of those very rare instances where I trust the prose immediately—I want to hurry forward and at the same time stay back and linger.

Before I'd even finished the first chapter, I knew that this was not just a another well-written memoir. It was something over and above, a kind of gate onto a world at once anchored in actual events of history and existing at the same time as its own universe. I couldn't believe that the book had remained so quietly on the shelf next to *Lolita* and *Pnin* and *Pale Fire*—that I had for so long been unaware of the extraordinary expressive power compressed between its covers. But isn't that how it always goes? I sit here now with books all around me, and any one of them could hold the next awakening.

I've gone back to *Speak, Memory* a number of times since that first reading, and it has been a different book every time. This is a familiar pronouncement, almost a cliché, I know. A book is like the Heraclitan river—you can't find yourself in the same one twice. The contents always seem different, nothing is as you remember. Books change as their readers change. The greater the interval between readings, the more the contents have been altered. When I read it again recently, it was through the eyes of a grown man, one who himself had been writing for many years.

.

I should probably say a few words about the person who has kept returning to this book. Who is he? Any attempt at self-characterization brings up the memoir question in miniature. But I won't start in on that just yet. In any case, I don't have the space here to provide more than an index-card's worth of self-assessment, but since any reading of a book is a two-sided encounter, I should at least offer that much.

While I am not a full-blown time-obsessive like Nabokov, I am an obsessive of my own stripe. From my earliest days, I've been preoccupied by thoughts about time—time passing, time standing still, moving one way out in the world and quite another inwardly. It is invisible but all-determining, measureable and not. For me, just contemplating the basic concepts of past, present, and future can bring on vertigo. But I also can't not ponder them—the tenses are profound and they fascinate me. In fact, I realized just now that I began one of the first essays I ever wrote with the sentence: "Time is the bone I've been gnawing all my life." I am gnawing still.

I can still remember the feeling of some of my earliest speculations—I imagine every child has them. How could it be that the universe had no end? How could the world go on forever? As we grow up, that most basic wondering gets pushed to the side—but it does not go away, the questions remain unanswered. I don't know how any of us ever deal with the concepts of infinity and eternity. For me those two mysteries were linked from the first, long before I ever heard the term *space-time continuum*—a concept, I'll confess, I can't even now begin to grasp.

Eternity and infinity are, of course, somehow grander and more forbidding terms than mere time and space. I stayed with the humbler pair, and between the two concepts, I found that time was somehow more compelling. I could make myself anxious just by contemplating the play of tenses. *One day I'll be a grown-up,* I would think, *then an old man. One day I will die.* Working in just one direction, toward the future, I could only think so far before everything got blurry. As it blurs now, sixty years later, though now the confusion extends into the past as well as the future. *Imagine: I was once a child, just starting out, and wondering what would become of me . . .* What happens to such intensities of thought? It could be they just go back into time itself, with memory as a means of access.

Unanswerable questions and intangible projections like these are the very foundation of my subjectivity. They have a great effect on my outlook on the world, and they have certainly shaped me as a reader. In fact, I would go so far as to say that it is reading—the act of it—that brings me closer to the mystery. Maybe that was why I became so devoted. From childhood on, novels especially have served as a conjuring tool for me, a spur to all kinds of imaginings. At the same time, they are a way of pinching vast chronologies between thumb and forefinger. As if by reading I can own that particular time-space continuum by proxy.

A novel scales the immensity of the world down into proportions we can grasp. And it was fiction that I tried my hand at first. The manipulation of tenses, and the variations of syntax—these create a heady illusion of control—not over real time, but over the narrative that serves as a time's surrogate. I also think that the desire to slow—if not actually arrest—the passing of time is for many of us a key reason for putting words on the page. Though there is no getting at time so long as one is *in* time, working with language can create a kind of psychological stasis, a place for Archimedes to stand.

I am still trying to account for why I was so susceptible to Nabokov's memoir on contact. Time was clearly involved. As soon as I opened *Speak, Memory*, and confronted the idea of a person's life as a "cradle rocking above an abyss," and existence as "but a brief crack of light between two eternities of darkness," the nerve was touched. From that point on, for Nabokov—and certainly for me, his reader—all contemplations of time were finally efforts to understand that narrow bright interval. How was it that our complex and perfectly specific world could have emerged from all that nothing? Nabokov's view of things was very much in sync with my way of contemplating the world.

Of course, there are many other reasons why I was so

taken, and I can identify some of them. Right alongside the power of that first vividly visual conception—an integral part of it—there was the utterly unique character of the prose. This, I thought as I started to read, is *it*. I saw, maybe as never before, how a writer's style could bring together so many registers of expression: the intimate, philosophical, comic, sensory, and metaphoric. Their completely unpredictable melding led me from sentence to sentence in a state of aesthetic anticipation. I was always wondering: what will be the next turn, the next surprise? Nabokov's own phrase for what he sought in writing was "aesthetic bliss."

The thrill I experienced from that style has never waned for me. On each return to the memoir, I find there are new facets catching the light, subtleties I had not noticed, or maybe had not been ready to notice. I don't just mean suggestive syntactical cues and telling instances of diction. I also mean a deeper understanding of how intimately the style is wedded to what it is expressing. So much of which, in the case of Nabokov, is, under transparent concealment, an abiding sorrow over a lost world.

I should mention another, different, reason for my fixation on *Speak, Memory*. Years after my earlier readings, I went back to the book once again. At this point, I was starting to work on my own memoir. I'm not sure what I was looking for that time besides stylistic inspiration—which I already knew I would find there and which I siphoned off greedily. But as I read, I also understood what it was I really needed. It's as if my unconscious had sent me back for instruction. I needed the courage of my subjectivity. I needed to believe that my own perceptions and memories—their scale and particularity—would show me the way.

This remains for me one of the main Nabokov lessons—that the importance of events in memoir is not to be determined by the usual standards of sequence or accepted hierarchies of mattering. It's all about the truth of one's own feeling. If a memory of a chance encounter or the breaking of a special toy has remained vivid over time, then that is to be considered—never mind what supposedly "important" things were going on at the time. Memory, for Nabokov, proposed the true scale of mattering. His immersion in his own past woke me up to the profundity of those endless layers of childhood, where, deep down, some of our keenest awakenings are to be found. He not only confirmed the importance of detail, but—no less important—also suggested the narrative means whereby one could move back and forth in the time of his life, exploiting the linkages that only hindsight could provide.

As I absorbed Nabokov's subjective presentation this last time, different perspectives came into view. I recognized more clearly than I had before that there was also the big picture—less obvious, but no less vital. Where I had read the memoir before with my antennae out for Nabokov's intricate interior stagings, now I also began to see how history, though relegated mostly to the background, nevertheless insinuated itself at every point. It was inescapable. The family's social standing under one political order was what allowed Nabokov his highly privileged childhood, while the overthrow of that order threw him into exile and psychologically severed his life. History was, in truth, the mover of everything, the so-called "first cause."

Seeing this now, I could fasten on any number of "signifying" moments that remind the reader of the larger context. Nabokov often used specific memories of family members (especially of his father) to illuminate the role of public events, how they determined decisions that he had been largely unaware of at the time. I also understood that, artistically speaking, he needed to convey his lack of that awareness in order to skew the traditional hindsight perspective and keep a hold on the subjective feel of his childhood.

For me, there was also a family connection to this same history, a connection that seemed less important when I was a younger reader, but which now, at certain points in the memoir, was striking to me.

Both my parents were born in Riga, Latvia, a quarter century after Nabokov's birth. Their lives, too, had been shaped by exile—first to Germany, then America. Reading *Speak, Memory,* I had felt a general connection from the first, but that connection grew much deeper when I recently came upon papers relating to my father's father. As it turns out, he had spent several years in Russia as a young man. He had been an anti-Tsar activist, writer, and was briefly imprisoned for being an agitator. Now, looking closer, I realized that my grandfather and Nabokov's father—also liberal, activist, lawyer, writer and imprisoned agitator—had been fighting the same cause at the same time in the same part of the world. This was 1905, the year of the first revolutionary activity. I was able to picture them moving in parallel through the same circuit.

Vladimir Nabokov's
Speak, Memory

Nabokov's Memoir

SPEAK, MEMORY, SUBTITLED *AN AUTOBIOGRAPHY Revisited*, was never a book written in consecutive sequence as a memoir. It was, as Nabokov makes clear in his Foreword, written piecemeal, in no chronological order, and assembled later. The earliest part appeared in print in 1943 and the last in 1950. The book was published first in 1951 as *Conclusive Evidence*, and then in revised form as *Speak, Memory* in 1960. The subtitle, I think, refers to that revision. What was the nature of the revision? I don't know. My own copy of the memoir is a yet further revised edition published in 1966. It's not completely clear how much tailoring was needed to bring it to its final state, but it might have been considerable.

Nabokov claims in his Foreword that while the chapters were written over a span of years, "they had been neatly filling numbered gaps in my mind which followed the present order of chapters." That sounds so highly controlled, and Nabokov was nothing if not that. But at times I call to mind an especially lyrical moment from *Lolita,* where Humbert

Humbert, the narrator, looks back on his past. "The days of my youth," he declares, "seem to fly away from me in a flurry of pale repetitive scraps like those morning snow storms of tissue paper that a train passenger sees whirling in the wake of the observation car." Trains, as we will see, are a kind of narrative trope for this writer.

Flying scraps of tissue can hardly serve as the basis for constructing a memoir, but even as I grant Nabokov his meticulous mode of bringing together his various experiences, I can't lose my sense that the past is also a tumult of associations.

Nabokov's younger-to-older chronology is definitely not of the standard sequential sort. In fact, his approach to subject and event is surprisingly radical—especially, as I've said, in its manipulation of scale. At one point he might re-create in close detail an afternoon of butterfly hunting, and then, just like that, in passing, make oblique reference to some major event taking place on the historical stage. He is a master of deliberate subjective disproportion.

In certain key instances, Nabokov deploys a strategy similar to the one Virginia Woolf uses in *To the Lighthouse*, where, in a short neutrally narrated section entitled "Time Passes," years are seen to pass by swiftly, even as minute interior details inside an empty house are itemized. At one point, without any inflection of emphasis, Woolf informs the reader—inside parentheses and with no affect—that Mrs. Ramsay, the woman who has been at the novel's center, had died one night years ago. Full stop. The abbreviated statement of fact is, of course, meant to detonate slowly, to open up a void in which her absence resonates even years later in the lives of her family.

I'm not sure that Nabokov in every case intended his omissions and understatements to have such ironic magnifying effect. They may also reflect the natural and universal solipsism of youth. Sequestered as he was on the family estate, Nabokov most likely had no immediate awareness of the growing tensions and flare-ups that would lead to the Revolution—even though his father was a government official deeply involved in the events of his time.

While basically moving forward in time, *Speak, Memory* proposes no straight biographical causality. Scenes follow scenes, often without any obvious links, as if one were haphazardly turning the pages of an old family photo album. Most of the lyrical first two thirds of the memoir comprise impressions from early childhood—extended portraits of tutors and governesses, young adult infatuations, as well as the scene of his very first writing inspiration. The last two chapters give us greatly elided snippets from his years at Cambridge, glimpses of the Russian expatriate community in Berlin, and then, after a great leap forward, a section where Nabokov, with his wife Vera and son Dmitri, are in Biarritz awaiting for their visa to be granted so they can emigrate to America. There is no sustained narrative to follow, only these loosely sequenced scenes and portraits. But the reader caught in the meshes of this most idiosyncratic narration can't but keep turning the pages.

Childhood and Memory

TO BE PRECISE ABOUT TIME—as one should with a writer as time-driven as Nabokov—*Speak, Memory* covers the period stretching from several days before Nabokov's birth in 1899 to 1940, when he and his wife and child finally receive their immigration papers for America. After the highly-intense focus of the childhood and youth chapters, the pages that follow—Cambridge, Berlin, and Biarritz—feel a bit like a coda. The pace changes. Major life-events (marriage, fatherhood) are omitted or referenced only in a sidelong way, and the almost hypnotic feeling of sustained duration that had dominated the earlier chapters tapers away. I accept the shift as Nabokov's way underscoring that childhood and youth are now set apart from the life that follows.

Nabokov is, as we know, the lyrical arch-nostalgist—though, of course, all nostalgia is fundamentally lyric in its nature. He gives us his recollections of a loved person, or place, in such an intimate way that we can almost feel the imminence of the losses to come. Or is it that we readers, who at least know about Nabokov's exile, fill in that melancholic shadow ourselves? I beleive I feel it in the prose, the turns of phrase, though I am also aware of factoring in what I know.

Childhood, the first world, is Nabokov's most natural subject and the book's subjective center, and it is the work of his memoir to bring it back to life. The attempt at resurrection is not just an exterior evocation, though it is very successfully that—it is also Nabokov's ardent effort to repossess the feeling of his inner life.

What Nabokov gives us, especially through the first few chapters, is a rich and multi-angled phenomenology of inner development. He does not go as far as James Joyce does in his *A Portrait of the Artist as a Young Man,* which begins with the child-voice declaiming: "Once upon a time and a very good time it was there was a moocow coming down the road . . ." Rather, Nabokov looks to evoke the successive perceptual stages of the growing child from hindsight vantage. It's an interesting fusion, the naïve *before* presented through the filter of the sophisticated *after.* The strategy allows Nabokov to use the full range of his developed gifts.

For a writer obsessed with time and memory, the plumbing of earliest memories offers an almost irresistible challenge. Nabokov can't resist. From his first few paragraphs—which have him marveling at the fact that the world existed before he was born—he goes in search of the very roots of awareness and consciousness.

He starts by proposing that the first stages of consciousness are "a series of spaced flashes," with the dark intervals between growing shorter and shorter, "until bright blocks of perception are formed, affording memory a slippery hold." He enacts this by offering at first intermittent blurry moments of memory, only later reaching the awareness of a continuous self.

The first of these "flashes" is his recognition, at age four, that the two people who he remembers standing on each side of him and holding his hands, are his mother and father. There is not much more to present, but there doesn't need to be. His point here is literally existential. He is marking this as the real beginning of consciousness, merging perception with recognition, and then retrospectively declaring: "from the present ridge of remote, isolated, almost uninhabited time, I see my diminutive self as celebrating, on that August day of 1903, the birth of sentient life."

Once that source point has been plotted, Nabokov can—and will for many chapters—immerse us in the sensations of his growing awareness. He does this by way of a finely-honed sensory accuracy. It's as if he can, via his adult insight, work his way back into what were some of the purest and as yet unself-conscious moments, giving us the double perspective of both "then" and "now," which is how the alchemy of memory works.

Following that first almost primordial recognition of his mother and father, Nabokov creates a scene of playing behind "a big cretonne-covered divan, white with black trefoils," asserting that, for him, history begins "not far from one end of this divan, where a large potted hydrangea shrub, with pale blue blossoms and some greenish ones, half conceals, in a corner of the room, the pedestal of a marble bust of Diana." By "history" he now means that basic continuity of awareness. Perception and consciousness are entwined in this moment, as they will be entwined from this point on.

Virginia Woolf—who in ways worked in the same key signature as Nabokov, who was also under the compulsion of time and memory—presented a similar instance in her autobiographical—and distinctly phenomenological—essay, "Moments of Being." There she charges up the most prosaic and trivial of early sensations with the urgency of recovery, as if these and these alone were the key to her innermost self. Of her first memory, she writes: "It is of lying half asleep, half awake, in bed in the nursery at St. Ives. It is of hearing waves breaking, one, two, one, two, and of sending a splash of water over the beach; and then breaking, one, two, one, two, behind a yellow blind. It is of hearing the blind draw its little acorn across the floor as the wind blew the blind out." She calls this memory the "base" that her life stands on. Likely we can all get back to some "first" moment. I myself remember sitting on the carpet in an apartment that I have but the vaguest sense of, taking in the silhouette of a sharp angle of what I will later fill in is my father's drafting table against the sun. These primary perceptions have a monumental status in one's private history. They mark the first recovered connection to the world.

I've never believed that childhood, however we demarcate it, is just an undeveloped version of the mature self. It is, without question, a condition of its own. Our early years are studded with first-time perceptions, intimately attuned to surroundings and saturated with detail. The child has a far more active sense of immediacy than the adult. The child also lives much of the time in a state of duration, away from the organizational tyranny of clock-time. Alas, this has to change, and the change marks a defeat. How not to think of Wordsworth's Intimations Ode, where he laments how the "shades of the prison-house" close upon "the growing boy."

Just as apt would be the romantic but also gloomy sway of Dylan Thomas's "Fern Hill," which first sets out the dreamy and sensory first world, "Time let me play and be / Golden in the mercy of his means" and then concludes with "Time held me green and dying / though I sang in my chains like the sea." What could be more poignant?

The loss of childhood is itself cause for a kind of mourning, one that can go on a whole life long. But for Nabokov, who certainly was of a temperament to succumb, that disinheritance is followed by another. The coming of the Revolution in 1917, and the family's forced exile finishes what growing up started, stripping him of the place of his growing up—home—and every last outward connection to his life before.

Nabokov's boyhood and early coming-of-age are the core of *Speak, Memory*, and the countering of their loss by way of memory is paramount. His deep sadness—indirect but steady—is felt throughout. As refracted images are sometimes more evocative than those directly seen, so, in this case, the greater emotion is felt not through active expressions of lament, but rather through the writer's most careful re-creation of the gone world. Every detail is presented in such a way that we know it has been relived—it evokes. The intense concentration of the work is almost a fulfillment in itself, proof of a successful re-immersion, if not the ultimately desired recovery.

•

What distinguishes Nabokov's portrayal of childhood and youth from portrayals in other memoirs is the fact that very little happens—narratively, I mean. There are really no sustained "stories," and few elements linking one passage to another. The whole memoir is episodic and associative in this way—it is plotless, a deliberate rejection of received forms. Nabokov doesn't present his experience according to literary expectations. We find very little tying up of threads, and almost no sense of this following that or of life-lessons being learned. Instead, he focuses a great deal on people, often creating character sketches in which he himself features as a fairly dim background figure. And who are these people around him? Tutors, governesses, members of the estate staff. They occupy much of the foreground, while members of his family are mostly kept off-stage. This creates an odd effect, as if we were looking at the back of a tapestry, trying to make out the outlines of the other side from the evidence of threads.

So it happens that his mother gets a few more intimate scenes while his father stays mostly in the distance, often in his public guise as estate owner and civil official. What prompted this choice of presentation? It may have been Nabokov's intent to accurately reflect his main boyhood interactions and attachments—his pampered existence had him mainly in the care of nannies, governesses, and tutors. Or else—and I'll come back to this—the skewed proportions might reflect his natural desire to protect their privacy, even as he knows that the narrative can't *not* include them.

I believe both explanations are true, but at this moment I might give slightly more weight to the first explanation: that Nabokov was taking on a unique writing challenge: looking to stay absolutely true to subjective impressions of his childhood as remembered it. Nabokov's parents are not prominently portrayed because in significant ways they were not that often immediately on stage. Vyra was a large working estate and familial arrangements were different in those times. As material things are presented throughout in terms of their subjective importance, the same might be true of the people who populated his younger life. Nabokov probably did spend more time with his governess Mademoiselle than most anyone else. She gets the bulk of a whole chapter to herself and Nabokov's descriptions of her are fondly attentive and feature some of his most evocative prose.

Any memoir is the final result of so many deliberations,

some small and some major, all of them decisive in terms of the integrity of the final product. Try writing a memoir and you will find this out very quickly. The questions come up immediately. What am I writing toward? What is my slant, what prompts me? Who should I include? What scenes should I focus on? And how much, I would ask—though there's no way to measure—is my unconscious dictating my choices?

These key decisions were hard for me. For when I stepped back and reflected on the whole of my experience, it seemed there was an angle from which any event or person was important. I felt some of the same confusion that I feel when cleaning a storage room or trying to winnow my bookshelves. I don't know how to judge, which is to say that I don't know how to read the future. Everything is contingent, always the *what if*? What if I one day need to refer to my old college notebooks, or use those perfectly good handweights . . . ? I might still find my way to medieval history. With writing memoir, I feel like I can imagine a use for any part of my past. So which to choose? There is no option to *not* choose.

When I reach that point, there is usually nothing to do but to run a version of the old pretend scenario, something to the effect of—*Quick! The house is on fire! You have ten minutes—what do you save?* The writing a life offers no such calamity—but by provoking yourself with such hyped-up urgency, you might discover what is urging you to write. Which scenes from your life are you most intent on saving?

My fire-rescue scenario is hyperbolic, of course, but the basic logic applies. As Ezra Pound wrote: "What thou lov'st well remains, the rest is dross." There's a good deal of wisdom in those nine words, a wisdom that gives the unconscious a significant role in the process. How can we know what it is we love—or at least deem essential? We can all name the obvious people and the special charged moments. But what about all the events and perceptions that are not outwardly significant or ostensibly valuable?

Elizabeth Bishop caught something of this split between inner and outer value in her poem "Crusoe in England." There she imagines the castaway rescued years later and returned to his home. "I'm old," says Crusoe.

I'm bored, too, drinking my real tea,
Surrounded by uninteresting lumber.
The knife there on the shelf—
It reeked of meaning like a crucifix.
It lived. How many years did I
Beg it, implore it, not to break?
I knew each nick and scratch by heart,
The bluish blade, the broken tip,
The lines of wood-grain on the handle . . .
Now it won't look at me at all.
The living soul has dribbled away.

Bishop is showing us a living past now gone dead, but doing so by first reimagining that past's original vitality. She reveals the power and value of seeming incidentals, be they concrete objects or—as seen elsewhere in the poem—passing episodes that proved later to be dense with accrued association. As is obvious to Nabokov's reader, context is everything. Context creates importance, and it follows that context can also take it away.

*

Thinking along these lines, I decided that I would pursue my memoir project in a similar mode—working not by design so much as by following the subjective traces. If an event "felt" like it was important, never mind what that event was, then it stayed. Nabokov not only taught me this, but his example also gave me the courage to push in this direction. Of course, I knew before I started that I couldn't finally go the full Nabokovian distance.

•

This might be a place to ask about the working of memory, which is, as we know, a largely unconscious process. Nabokov's memoir testifies to this, as does the story of Marcel Proust's *petite madeleine* dipped in tea. What we learn from both is that the trigger doesn't matter nearly as much as the fact of the triggering, which then sets into motion the mysterious logistics of association.

In my own growing-up years, I know that I granted

the expected importance to the various keynote life-events: being inducted into the Boy Scouts, driving to California on a family vacation, building a rowboat (which promptly sank) with my friend. But what I discovered years later, looking back and writing about those times, was that while I could still remember the events objectively, they had left in me almost no subjective trace. At the same time, I could still feel the furtive thrill of squeezing through a hole in a fence and trespassing on a neighboring farm. I could also feel the heat in the room and see the inert shape on the board when we gathered to watch the dissection of a white rat in science class; I remember so clearly having to go into the hall, pressing my back hard against the cool wall . . . What *is* the stuff of a life?

One of the main mysteries has to do with the editorial function of the unconscious—how it dictates subjective mattering, what fades and what remains. But also: how it can happen that we sometimes linger on a seemingly incidental memory and find it gradually yielding up certain long-forgotten details and then revealing a whole associative trail. Again, what matters, and—crucially—why? While I was working on my memoir, I sometimes felt like the movie detective staring long and hard at the evidence pinned to his corkboard, waiting to see if some clue might "speak" and reveal a direction. Such staring is unfocused; it is a purely unconscious process.

If I were to pursue this line of thinking to its ultimate ends, I might end up proposing that it is finally the unconscious alone that writes this kind of memoir—that it is, in the last analysis, the sole arbiter of mattering. Memory is its agency, memoir its legacy. But the unconscious can't do all the work. The material as it emerges is often without any context or narrative coherence. It is a chaos of sensation and fragments of incident. To even begin, the memoirist has to think toward a shape. This means figuring out all sorts of things, including sequence and scale. Every memoir, Nabokov's included, emerges out of a complex negotiation between emerging content and the form-giving imperative.

Because it proceeds the way it does, by private predilection, following the trail of Nabokov's own real affinities, I feel a good deal closer to *Speak, Memory* than I do to more obviously arranged recollections. I trust Nabokov's voice. The sentences themselves are, it's true, highly wrought and make use of a great deal of artifice, but the details have such absolute-seeming accuracy that I am persuaded by them. This, I sometimes think when I'm reading, is how the experience—whatever it was—had to be presented. Given the accumulation of so many fresh and immediate details and sharply rendered moments, I can't help but be taken inside his way of looking. This uncanny transposition of the reader's mind into the narrator's is what most writers strive to achieve, not that many reach a level as intimate as what Nabokov achieves.

Here is a sample passage comprising a series of images that arrive through the scrim of fond memory—one of those occasions when we see Nabokov at a high sparkle:

I see with the utmost clarity the sun-spangled
river; the bridge, the dazzling tin of a can left by a
fisherman on its wooden railing ... the stone building of the new house near the wooden old one; and,
as we swiftly drove by, the little black dog with very
white teeth that dashed out from among the cottages at a terrific pace ...

This is, even in slightly abridged form, a true
Nabokovian action-shot, a moving pan of countryside
orchestrated and paced by generous use of semi-colons.
To me, it feels less like an immediately transcribed memory than a construction made out of remembered things,
which poses an epistemological conundrum about authenticity versus artifice. Does an assembled patchwork memory have the same status as a naturally recollected scene?
Many would say no, of course. But I believe that what the
memoirist is out to capture is the spirit and emotion of the
bygone event, and that artistic shaping done in the service
of "how it was" is just as valid.

In this passage, the selected details are carefully worked
together so as to involve us in the immediate action, and in
terms of sensory evocation they do. But for me it's finally his
noting the dog's "very white teeth" that certifies the scene.
Its vivid unexpectedness assures me that Nabokov was working from deep inside the memory. This is a child's perception recovered and not a grown man's imagining. It can be
seen as a literary instance of what Roland Barthes called the

punctum in a photograph: that half-hidden and unplanned anomaly that confirms the reality of the moment.

The Family

DIVERGING FROM THE MORE CONVENTIONAL presentation of parents in memoir—as exemplars or antagonists—Nabokov, as I suggested, situates his own mother and father mainly in the background. Though this is mainly a coming-of-age memoir, his parents don't much affect his experiences as he narrates them. Nabokov does not disclose any real struggles, and maybe there weren't any. The skeptical reader naturally assumes that if struggles did exist—and how could they *not*—they have either been sublimated to become occasional implications, or else they appear indirectly, in variously refracted forms.

This last suggestion would probably be unacceptable to Nabokov, who has so often in his writings mocked Freud and his theorizing of our inner workings. Though I sometimes think that his loud objections to any science of psychology were given more for effect—as a kind of artistically-entitled crankiness—than as an honest repudiation. For as we see, his memoir—indeed all his work—conveys the shrewdest psychological understandings, except they are not codified or set out as a theory. The difference, and the deeper point of contention, is that in developing his theories, Freud, a scientist, always sought to generalize and find an underlying principlej. Nabokov, for his part, abhorred any generalization and never wavered from his belief in the uniqueness of all things and the singularity of every human destiny.

THE FATHER

Nabokov's father—his namesake—first appears in that

moment that Nabokov's calls his earliest memory of his parents as separate beings. He sets it up like a photograph. His father is remembered as a stiffly-posed figure in uniform. He and Nabokov's mother are each holding one of the boy's hands. That original impression is never really countered—it is an emblem of his old-world upbringing. His father is a taciturn man—we presume this from the absence of any real speaking parts. He is shown to be formal in an old-school way, and most mentions of him are brief, and usually involve him acting in some official capacity. He was, after all, an important government figure, and the patriarchal master of the vast family estate.

The one, maybe only, telling exception—a deliberate counter to this presentation—comes very early on in the very first chapter. Young Nabokov, sitting in the dining room and looking out the window, has what feels like a surreal vision:

> From my place at the table I would suddenly see through one of the west windows a marvelous case of levitation. There, for an instant, the figure of my father in his wind-rippled summer suit would be displayed, gloriously sprawling in midair. His limbs in a curiously casual attitude, his handsome, imperturbable features turned to the sky.

The workers on his estate are just outside, flinging his father up from a blanket they've stretched into a kind of trampoline. Something is being celebrated. There is "levity" in the scene, but it also goes deeper. Nabokov ends the passage with an elaborated simile, in which the father aloft is imagined as "one of those paradisiac personages who comfortably soar, with such a wealth of folds in their garments, on the vaulted ceilings of a church . . ."

This is, of course, the impression of the credulous child, but as filtered by an imaginative artist through a half-century's hindsight. And then, as so often with Nabokov, there is yet another turn of the handle. The building sentence continues: ". . . while below, one by one, the wax tapers in mortal hands light up . . . and the priest chants of eternal repose, and funeral lilies conceal the face of whoever lies there, among the swimming lights, in the open coffin." What a wide swing this is—from the buoyant "flying" to the image of the inert body in its coffin. That image is, as will come clear, part of Nabokov's oblique but ongoing treatment of the death of his father years later. The fact that the visual closes the first chapter underscores its importance to the memoir. For by literary law, whenever a chapter concludes in this way, the words are meant to linger on in the silence.

Though there are no extended one-on-one scenes between father and son, and only a few moments where their paths are seen to cross, we do get brief reports about the father's political involvement, and how his views and writings insured the family's exile at the time of the Revolution. But it is really only through the staged presentation of his father's death years later that Nabokov conveys his complex relation to the man.

The way Nabokov does this is a perfect instance of his way of breaking up sequence and chronology for his own ends. Early on in the memoir—and quite unexpectedly—he plants separate time markers for the eventual deaths of both of his parents. He freely manipulates time, as is his wont, shuttling back-and-forth between tenses and time zones. The eventual narration of his father's death is a *tour de force* of indirection.

Nabokov begins that half-buried narrative with a recollection of a Christmas Eve in childhood, when he and his brother Sergei are instructed by their mother *not* to look in their Christmas stockings until the next day. Of course they disobey and look to see what they will get. The next day, having rewrapped and replaced the little packages, the brothers feign surprise for the sake of their mother. She realizes the deceit and bursts into tears. The scene ends.

But then, without even starting a new paragraph—and with an unsettling terseness—Nabokov writes:

A decade passed. World War One started. A crowd of patriots and my Uncle Ruka stoned the German Embassy. *Petersburg* was sunk to *Petrograd* against all rules of nomenclatural priority . . .

The newsreel sampler of the times follows, into which Nabokov inserts a casual mention of his mother's eventual exile to Germany—the subtlest of hints. Then he is back to his recollections from childhood, this time describing the various dogs that had been in the family. "Sometime in 1904," he begins, "my father bought at a dog show in Munich . . ." and ends the paragraph memorializing the "final dachshund," which followed them into exile. He uses the dogs to project his condensed history forward into the 1930s, whereupon he suddenly appears before us as an adult. He is making a visit to Prague, where, he notes, "my widowed mother spent her last years." His father's death is, again, brought up by implication.

But there are, of course, several more turns to come. In the very next paragraph, making another knight's move in time and space, Nabokov describes how he and his brother, on holiday from Cambridge University, visit their mother, who is then living in Berlin. It is now 1922 and this little scene marks what will prove to be a great family tragedy:

> I happened to be reading to her Blok's verse on Italy—had just gotten to the end of the little poem about Florence, which Blok compares to the delicate, smoky bloom of an Iris, and she was saying over her knitting, "Yes, yes, Florence does look like a *dimniy iris*, how true! I remember—" When the phone rang.

". . . the phone rang." Nothing more is said, nor maybe needs to be. We hear no more about the call, and the very next paragraph, interestingly, comprises another of Nabokov's compressed chronologies, this one describing his mother's life after the call, but without ever mentioning the death of her husband. He does finally note that his mother died in Prague on the eve of World War Two. Both deaths are given the sparest presentation, and this raises questions.

I can think of no other memoirist who would dare such a maneuver, breaking out of one narrative time frame like that to do a mash-up of European history, mention indirectly his mother's death, and then return to that former frame. Doing this, Nabokov reminds us, as he does on occasion, that his writer's vantage lets him preside over the whole of his experience, from earliest origins to the reflections from the time of the writing.

This zigzag narration does not conform to the literary-aesthetic standards of the day. A gatekeeping guardian would probably pronounce these paragraphs a botch. And I understand. Years of teaching allow me to imagine I'm grading the work of my student, the young Nabokov. Reading, I find myself completely exasperated. *These scenes need transition,* I scrawl in the margin. *Do not fly around in time like this! First show reaction to news of father's death . . .* I would tell the young man to rewrite.

But this then raises the question about earning permission. Can it be that what I would flag as student's jumble of time frames can through another lens be seen as an act of daring—a bold subversion of traditional ways? I think it can, though I offer no logical support. But I do know how I will on occasion extend aesthetic tolerance, and then, often as not, find I was justified in doing so. If I trust the writer,

I often see that his move has stretched my perspective. But I do at times also wonder whether this tolerance isn't just playing into the "genius" game, the assertion of which has Picasso saying "If I spit, it's art."

With Nabokov's treatment of his father, I reserve judgment; I wait to see if his presentation is not part of a strategy. Is it a calculated previewing of an event ahead of time? Believing that Nabokov writes every sentence with full intention, I feel corroborated when I find another such instance just a few pages on, one that yet again overturns our sense of narrative time.

The set-up involves a duel—and how Russian that is! The year is 1911 and with the scene he is back in his boyhood days. His father has just been insulted by a member of the rightest press, and a challenge has been offered. Nabokov has been raised on the romanticized stories of Lermontov's and Pushkin's duels of honor, and they thrill him. But this is his own father and he's naturally anxious and afraid. Unable to detach himself, he admits that "behind it all was yet a very special emotional abyss that I was trying to skirt," by which he means "the tender friendship underlying my respect for my father . . ."

This sidelong reflection is inserted into a scene of Nabokov racing home to find out about the arrangements for the duel. He is charged up and tense, but as soon as he steps into the vestibule, all he hears are loud cheerful voices. "I knew at once that there would be no duel," he writes, "that the challenge had been met by an apology, that all was right."

But then, unexpectedly, he writes:

I could not look at my father. And then it happened: my heart welled in me like that wave . . . and I had no handkerchief, and ten years were to pass before a certain night in 1922, at a public lecture in Berlin, when my father shielded the lecturer (his old friend Milyukov) from the bullets of two Russian Fascists and was fatally shot . . . But no shadow was cast by that future event upon the bright stairs of our St. Petersburg house . . . and several lines of play in a difficult chess composition were not yet blended on the board.

This is the strongest expression in the memoir of Nabokov's feeling for his father—he never again comes close. Considering his aesthetics of emotional reticence, it's easy to assume powerful underlying emotion. The sentences barely conceal a brooding sadness. The passage already contains the knowledge of his father's date of dying. On a more cerebral level, I'm intrigued to see him applying the analogy of chess to the working out of human circumstance.

The "lines of play" referenced suggests that there is for all of us an array of possible courses, but also, I think, that as the game proceeds our choices narrow us down into inevitability, what might be called our fate. Nabokov is a writer so preoccupied with outcomes that his father's death can also be seen as a philosophical test-case. Did he die as he did because of the myriad choices he made? Was that his destiny, or just the result of an unhappy convergence of events, none of which could have been foreseen? I don't know that Nabokov's outlook on life, which includes a faith in deep patternings, would have accepted that chance alone brought about that tragic event.

THE MOTHER

Nabokov's way of writing about his mother—his stance toward her—is quite different. Their interchanges are calm and tender, and almost always take place in a context of warm domesticity. Mother and son play cards together, read to one another, and exchange confidences. In such scenes as we have, she is receptive to the boy's attentions. Early on in the memoir, she imparts to him her outlook on the world:

> To love with all one's soul and to leave the rest to fate, was the simple rule she heeded. "*Vot zapomni* [now remember] she would say in conspiratorial tones as she drew my attention to this or that loved thing in Vyra—a lark ascending the curds-and-whey sky of a dull spring day, heat lightning taking pictures of a distant line of trees in the night . . .

The tone here immediately breaches distance. The opening phrase, "to love with all one's soul," sets the emotional key signature. We understand right away that mother and son are quite comfortable with each other. The use of such precise details and images, moreover, joins them together by way of shared perception. They are contemplating the same specific things, all of them poetic in nature. This is most obviously an affective bond. Finally—and this is something we see in other passages involving mother and son—is Nabokov's use of a Russian phrase, a snippet of the "mother" tongue. Subliminally, but effectively, it joins them together in their home language.

It's surprising, then, that the mother's death, like the father's, is treated from such a distance. There is the protective reticence, we grant that, but we might also keep in mind how once the Russian homeland has been left behind, absolutely everything in the memoir is seen as if from afar. The matter-of-fact mention of her death is not, I'm sure, a matter of emotional detachment. Might it also be a structural calculation? For if the deaths of his parents were given the emotional attention they deserve, the center of gravity of the whole project would have to shift.

One of the most important scenes between son and mother comes when he rushes to show her his very first poem. At this point, Nabokov is sixteen, and he has been completely caught up in the urgency of its composition—it is narrated as a quasi-mystical event. He has known nothing like it. His language and images fill him—he can't *not* compose. He works feverishly, and then, as soon as he has finished, he hurries to her room. She is there, reclined on her sofa and reading the newspaper.

"With a little cough," he writes, "I sat down on a

footstool and started my recitation." As he reads—this is very Nabokovian—he also notices the details of the daguerreo-types on the opposite wall. As he pauses at the last stanza, checking his memory, he hears his mother sniff. When he finishes the last lines he looks over at her:

> She was smiling ecstatically through the tears that streamed down her face. "How wonderful, how beautiful," she said, and with the tenderness in her smile still growing, she passed me a hand mirror . . . Looking into my own eyes I had the shocking sensa-tion of finding the mere dregs of my usual self, odds and ends of an evaporated identity which it took my reason quite an effort to gather again in the glass.

•

For any memoirist writing about others—and I say this with complete certainty—the closer the relationship, the more fraught things are apt to get. So many friendships and fami-lies have broken up over certain presentations, and not even necessarily vilifying ones. The main thing, of course, is the nature and quality of the portrayal. I have not had the "plea-sure" of finding myself in another's memoir, but it takes me no effort to imagine my likely reaction. *That's nothing like what happened! I never said that!* I can't imagine finding myself in a passage of a book where I would recognize myself approvingly. While I may go around every day in a subjective fog, not objectively at all vivid to myself, I would only have to meet my "objective" self on the page to know exactly how I was misrepresented. Is there any way not to be angered by the ceding of authority?

Then we have the obvious ethical question. What right does an author have to use another individual in a work of creative interpretation? This is wholly different from using her for documentary purposes—a magazine article, say—though we know that articles, too, can become matters of litigation. As regards memoir, the key word is "creative," which can't but suggest license. To be incorporated via whatever license into another's interpretive project is automatically disconcerting. For the person is not being just described and characterized—she is shown for who she is in relation to the subject. This means, quite simply, that the subject is divested of subjectivity and seen through the will of another. The presentation could be condemned as a kind of identity theft, though in this genre such theft is unavoidable; there could be no memoir if writing about others were not allowed. What is absolutely essential is the memoirist's discretion. Aware of the damage he could, even unwittingly, inflict, I believe Nabokov chose to honor the essential privacy of his immediate family.

Nabokov later uses the same kind of protective concealment for his wife, Vera. She is invoked—barely—in the later pages of the memoir, mostly as part of a "we," which also includes their son, Dimitry. The author has told us nothing whatsoever about their meeting or marriage or the birth of their child. Interestingly, though, as concerns Vera, he does something seemingly minor that is nonetheless worth pondering. A very few times, with no warning, he will abruptly turn from his narration in progress and address his wife. He does right near the end, at the beginning of Chapter 15, when he declares out of the blue: "The years are passing, my dear, and presently no one will know what you and I know. Our child is growing . . ."

As Vera figures so minimally in the memoir, the reader naturally does a double-take, wondering if there was something he might have missed. A thorough check confirms that there wasn't. But really, aside from that short disruption, the impact is finally minor. The few instances, coming only rarely and impinging on nothing in the immediate narration, are mostly forgotten. We move on. Except that now we have been reminded that there is a singular presence behind the wall of words—a man with a wife, a child, a real life.

Our surprise when we encounter it Nabokov's sudden addressing of Vera shows us how much of our reading of anything is contingent on our baseline assumptions. When these are undermined, we are unsettled, drawn out of our immersion. We are also made to recognize that we even had those assumptions. Who *did* we imagine the memoirist was speaking to? I usually assume that the intended audience is that generalized population: his readers past, present and future. Though I am momentarily surprised by his addressing Vera, I find that I do quite easily lapse back into my original unheeding assumption.

Exile

*. . . the unhealable rift forced between a human being
and his native place, between the self and a true home:
its essential sadness can never be surmounted.*

—EDWARD SAID

THERE IS NEVER A SINGLE key that can explain a writer's
output, but we right away recognize the most obvious shaping force behind Nabokov's work. It's the fact of exile. "Exile"
is a broad and general word, easily noted in a biographical
précis. But to the exiled one, it is a central life-changing event,
at once particular and metaphorical. For that person, home
is replaced by the memory of home. What had formerly just
been the ongoing circumstances of life are abruptly changed.
Suddenly, there is a before and after. That "before" then very
likely becomes the subject of the most intense memories,
many of which are saturated with longing.

"Nostalgia," often regarded as a minor-key emotion,
somewhat akin to sentimentality, is actually anything but
that. Etymologically it comes from the Greek *nostos*, which

means "the longing for home." What could be more profound? The whole core myth of Christianity is about exile, the loss of Eden—the ideal habitation—innocence vanished. Picture the broken posture and ravaged expressions of Adam and Eve in Masaccio's great painting *Expulsion*. Could there be a more powerful expression of grief?

For Nabokov, who was born right at the turn of the century, and who enjoyed an idyllic boyhood, growing up on a vast estate, a member of one of Russia's privileged and politically important families, the abrupt displacement by the Russian Revolution in 1917 was a trauma he tried to recover from for the rest of his life. The word "recover" can mean two very different things, and both apply. One has to do with the regaining of emotional equilibrium, the other with the artistic retrieval of what was lost. That dual compulsion is obviously the driving force behind Nabokov's intense and prolific expression. His elaborate and highly-wrought prose style, which can sometimes appear to be a gesture of detachment, is, paradoxically, a way for him to get closer to that lost past. Vibrant detail is the path of access, and Nabokov's way of making sentences allows him the sharpest sort of precision. A token of the exile's obsessive need to get it just right, it is rooted in loss.

I do understand at least a small part of this exile's urge to recollect and restore. It was also one of the incentives behind my own attempt at memoir, though at a generation's remove. Though my second-hand exposure to displacement and loss was not remotely comparable to what Nabokov knew, it did allow me to nonetheless engage more deeply what I was reading.

My parents, as I mentioned earlier, were born roughly twenty-five years after Nabokov, in Latvia, which was at that point not yet part of the Soviet empire. They both left their homes in their teens during the German occupation. Latvians at that time were allowed to take up residence in a displaced persons zone in southern Germany, which is where they met. Both were at that point emigres, and exiles. But when they came to America they were no longer emigres but immigrants. The shift is all important. The former looks back at what was left, the latter looks to the future. My parents married in 1950 in their new "home," and I was born the very next year.

The child of immigrants, I grew up in a Latvian-speaking home, and I really only picked up English once I started pre-school. This duality of languages has determined much about my way of looking at the world, including my sense of an inner split, and my penchant—though that may be too mild of a word—for contemplating the past. I trace many things in my life back to the home world, in which English was always somehow the "other," not completely real.

Immigrants though they were, much of the conversation in our family, at least as I selectively filtered it, was about "home"—their first home. My parents had both grown up in Riga, and though they did not meet until they were in Germany, Riga was the place of their intersecting memories.

These memories were often revisited, discussed, elaborated, or corrected. That corner by the park, those shops, school life, ice-skating . . . The past was brought up so often over time that I, too, started to recognize—which is to say *imagine*—what it was they were remembering. When, years later, not long before the fall of the Iron Curtain, I finally traveled to Riga with my parents. I felt a powerful and also strangely skewed sense of *déjà vu* almost as soon as we landed. My parents would point out this place and that, and each seemed so familiar that I felt like I was remembering it myself. Psychologically speaking, a great part of my visit was about adjusting the impressions I had conjured through my second-hand memory.

Elizabeth Bishop wrote with the most wrenching irony: "The art of losing isn't hard to master . . ." For Nabokov it was, and mastery, if even possible, would have to come via words on the page. I find no evidence that he believed that he might one day return. Had going back later become possible, I doubt that he would have made that decision. He would have known that major features of his former life had been destroyed or were greatly changed. The new Russia would be nothing like the brightly intimate version of the world he had re-created in his work. Going back would have tainted what he had so laboriously restored, forcing on him a secondary exile—this one from his own memories.

How could his created version withstand the glare of the present? While front and center in *Speak, Memory*, Nabokov's lost world is present in everything he wrote—if not literally, as direct subject, then in his tone, which is so tinged with melancholic nostalgia. That tone can be detected behind even his fondest descriptions—they are descriptions of what no longer is. Nabokov in his work depicts the longed-for thing as transformed by memory. As when he writes: "those exciting St. Petersburg mornings when the fierce and tender, damp and dazzling arctic spring bundled away broken ice down the sea-bright Neva!" Here is an instance where the joy of the language overpowers the fact of the loss, though that fact is what calls forth such invigorated expression.

Nostalgic recall allows not only an embellishing of certain details, but it also often discovers a particular cadence. We can hear it in writers as diverse as Andre Aciman, John Banville, Virginia Woolf, and Saul Bellow. They all write extended descriptive sentences that simulate the emotional nature of their remembering in the cadence. Memory does not come in terse or choppy modes—it is primarily emotional, and needs room to resonate. Simple declarative sentences just won't do.

By the same token, however, if a writer were to use this more indulgent mode of expression to depict of events in the near-present, he would quickly be accused of the sin of purple prose. And purple prose has a distinct and limited place on the spectrum of literary expression. It is overblown, often undisciplined, and only the assumption of deep longing allows it—and that only to master stylists and only in limited amounts.

Exile creates a gap, an existential division in the self.

It points to a literal banishment. It's true, obviously, that we are all in exile from the past, with memories the only breadcrumbs leading us back. "You can't go home again," wrote Thomas Wolfe. But for most of us, the door to our beginnings is closed quietly behind our backs, not slammed shut. What's more, most of us don't remark our pasts until later. The memories, the deeper sort, come long after the fact, and have acquired some potency in the interim. Literal exile, on the other hand, right away throws up a barrier that says "never again," driving home the idea of irrevocability in a soul-shaking way.

The pain and disruption of exile are one thing, and the making of a new life is another. When my parents left Germany and came to America, they set about starting their new lives. They were still in their early twenties, able to adapt more readily than older people. An architect by training, my father fell in with the new Modernist ethos and aesthetic. Modernism was a full about-face from the past. Everything was to be clean and unadorned; its underlying ethos was all about fresh beginnings after the war. In America this went hand in hand with the whole post-war boom.

There was, however, a psychological split in our family. We lived in a quasi-Modernist home and followed no Old World customs, except maybe at Christmas. We drove around in a Ford Fairlane, went skiing in winter and to the lake in summer. But surrounded as we were by the prosperous and forward-looking present, we nonetheless spoke only Latvian with each other. It was the home language, and speaking it, for my parents, kept the past alive. I came by my nostalgias at second hand, and in the face of all that was bright and new.

Nabokov, by his own admission, went through several major dislocations, and in *Speak, Memory* he uses the analogy of the dialectic to suggest how they determined the shape of his life. "The twenty years I spent in my native Russia," he writes, "take care of the thetic arc." His years of voluntary exile in Europe he deems the antithesis, and finally, "[T]he period spent in my adopted country forms a synthesis—and a new thesis."

It's surprising that a writer so deeply anti-Marxist as Nabokov would characterize his experience in terms of Hegel's dialectic, the structural base of Marxist theory—and the analogy does feel a bit forced, logically imposed. But it can be made to fit: *Speak, Memory* itself can be seen to be the fruit of that first synthesis, presenting the past as refracted through a sensibility that has incorporated both the thesis and antithesis.

By calling his life in America "a new thesis," Nabokov makes clear that exile had become a starting point for him and his family. And so it was. In his reborn life, he raised a family, taught at Wellesley College and Cornell, traveled to the West—for him a lepidopterist's paradise—and wrote prolifically in his second language. But as we know from *Speak, Memory*, no matter what steps he took to remake his life, the active core of his identity remained his Russian childhood.

Everyone's formational years make up their

psychological core. But though they are, in Virginia Woolf's words, "the base" on which everything rests, they are seldom presented in as determined a way as here. Nabokov applied his hypersensitivity to time to the trauma of loss in order to keep it live as the true center of his life. Of his university years in England, he writes that they were finally "the story of my trying to become a Russian writer." All the celebrated features of Cambridge—he lists "venerable elms, blazoned windows, loquacious tower clocks"—meant nothing except insofar as they framed and supported his "rich nostalgia."

Scales of Mattering

FOR ME, WRITING A MEMOIR was a late-breaking impulse that ended up taking over my life for several years. I'm not sure what the real trigger was. I can only say that as I closed in on my fifties—somewhat after the Dantean "middle of the journey"—I realized that I was thinking about my life in a whole new way. My past seemed to be taking on a new coloration, a changed optic. When I tried to explain the feeling of this sense of things to friends, I often spoke in terms of a kind of double-vision. It was, I said, as if a strip of celluloid—the film of my life thus far—had been folded over on itself. Everything that was happening seemed to have a kind of ghost outline behind it. I was experiencing all sorts of life-echoes and sensations of *déjà vu*.

I also felt as if my recognition of correspondences and patterns across time was moving me toward some new understanding. I wanted to write my way into these new sensations and memories—I wanted to write a memoir. But how to do this? How could I possibly capture so many layers of memory-time and render that four-dimensional sensation that comes with the infiltration of present by past, and at the same time get around the almost obligatory pull toward chronology?

I was confused. While I knew what my materials were, and I could feel the pressure to write building, I was still stymied by the structural *how*? I knew enough to know that in memoir everything depends on vantage and tone. And there was, of course, that bottom-line given: that only so many things can be included. Which ones to choose—the eternal challenge.

I stewed over these questions for some time. As an exercise I made myself imagine the book I wanted to write as a done thing. I pictured it between covers and on a bookstore shelf. What would be the feel of the prose, where would it start and end? I read many memoirs looking for cues. Frank Conroy's *Stop-Time* was, I remember, hugely influential. I liked his way of packaging eras of his life in discrete chapters, almost as if the memoir were a collection of stories with one recurring protagonist. Annie Dillard's *An American Childhood* showed her using scaled-down scenes and sharp sensory details to get close to the intimate textures of her childhood.

It was at about this time that I went back to *Speak, Memory*, which—as so often happens to me with books—I thought I knew quite well but had also forgotten. Also, I had never read it with my own memoir project in mind, and so this time my reading was different. *Speak, Memory* was a new book. I was surprised to see how inventively Nabokov achieved effects I hadn't paid much attention to before. For one thing, he had created for himself a supple structure of separate chapters which progressed episodically within a casual-feeling chronology, and of course I wondered how much this had to do with the fact that the pieces were originally written for separate occasions. I also saw more clearly than before how he used close-focus detail to create immediacy, and also how he used details and contexts to indicate what I have come to think of as the private scales of mattering. What an eye-opener!

Finishing the memoir, I wondered briefly why Nabokov chose to end where he did—in the south of France on the eve of departure to America. But it quickly came clear. His life began as if new—*as if*—in America, thus making 1940 a most convenient cutoff point. A cycle had been completed. For Nabokov, who was writing the book in America, the main work of remembrance was done; a cycle was complete. But some time later, as I was trying to bring my own memoir to some conclusion, I realized that he might have had another reason as well.

My original idea for a memoir had been to carry my "story" forward from childhood into the near-present. But every time I tried to wrap things up, I felt that something was wrong. My carefully planned-out chapter on marrying and starting a family—the projected conclusion—was not working at all with the chapters that came before. But reading Nabokov again, I understood. A big part of my impetus to write scenes from my younger years was to try to recreate some of the saturation of those times. Alas, my attempt to render my more recent "adult" years was working against that effect. As the British novelist L.P. Hartley wrote: "The past is a foreign country; they do things differently there."

Childhood especially has its own structure—it is a version of self that is nothing like the more socially-defined self that emerges later. And though Nabokov does at points flash forward in time, his meticulously detailed re-creation of childhood perception is intense enough to achieve the effect of an irretrievable past and also demonstrate the power of concentrated recollection. Times past recovered by way of the right evocative language are poignant; they might be as close as we can get to the past. Not just because the words allow us to experience the nuances of that perception, but also because presentation at that range encourages us to feel the moment from the inside, as a timeless-feeling duration. Sentence by sentence, I don't know that anyone excels Nabokov in this, maybe not even Proust.

I had found my guide and inspiration. What so compelled me was not only that Nabokov presented childhood time as we subjectively register it, but also that he was so alert to patterns *across* time. In *Speak, Memory* he gives the reader the sense that focusing on these patterns might lead to some kind of subjective breakthrough. As if a deeper understanding of our personal existence depended on assembling the pieces of the puzzle, patiently locking each to each. That analogy, as we'll see, is not far-fetched.

But Nabokov's memoir held something that was no less inspirational for me. For as I read, I began to see how the many variations in descriptive scale could be used to represent modulations of attention itself. This was major, and liberating. It underscored the idea that the perception was subjectively often more important than the thing perceived. *Speak, Memory* was asking me whether I dared to trust that subjectivity of memory completely. But what did such trust mean? If, for me, a memory of breaking a lamp in the living room loomed larger than televised reports of the Cuban Missile Crisis, would I render it so? I knew that there were reasons and considerations. That broken lamp might, after all, be the protruding thread of a larger story, something connected to my father's anger and, further, to the sudden changes of atmosphere at home. I could accept the logic of that, even though I couldn't give myself over to those memories as trustingly as Nabokov did.

One was what one remembered, not what one had learned or been told—Nabokov brought it home with such *éclat*. Part of my renewed interest in his memoir was in watching how he worked his strategies from page to page. Sometimes he would confront the reader with the outsized foregrounding of a seemingly "minor" detail. He might do this as a way of underscoring the intensity of the boy's interest in something particular (a toy train, say), and as an attempt to actually re-create that intensity. But sometimes it might also be Nabokov's discreet way of planting a detail to foreshadow something that will be important in the future.

We see a perfect instance of this early in the memoir in a scene that brings together the most subjective of recollections with a much larger moment, one that gives us a look at history from a very different vantage.

Nabokov is five years old at this point. The Russo-Japanese war is in progress, and though the boy thrills to the wartime photos his nursemaid shows him from an illustrated weekly, he has no larger sense of what is happening—how could he? But the adult Nabokov, living now in the land of hindsight, remembers when his father one afternoon brought him into his study to greet an old family friend, General Kuropatkin.

There, the general tries to amuse the boy with a little trick using ten matches. First he lays them end to end on the divan. That, he says, is the sea in calm weather. "Then he tipped up each pair so as to turn the straight line into a zigzag—and that was "a stormy sea." He is scrambling the matches and about to do another trick, when his aide-de-camp is shown into the room and bends to his ear. "With a Russian, flustered grunt," writes Nabokov, "Kuropatkin heavily rose from his seat, the loose matches jumping on the divan as his weight left it. That day he had been ordered to assume supreme command of the Russian Army in the Far East."

A remarkable telling by itself, juxtaposing the child's eye focus on the matches, and the historically significant fact of the general's assignment. The striking image of the matches jumping on the divan almost overshadows his later understanding of what had just transpired. But there's more. For as Nabokov reveals in the very next paragraph, there was a curious sequel to this moment. Some years later, he tells us, his father was in flight from the Bolsheviks who had taken over St. Petersburg. As he was crossing a bridge, he was accosted by "an old man who looked like a gray-bearded peasant in his sheepskin coat." The man asked his father for a light, and as they came closer, each recognized the other. Writes Nabokov: "I hope old Kuropatkin in his rustic disguise, managed to avoid Soviet imprisonment, but that is not the point." What has his attention here is the evolution of the match theme:

> those magic ones he had shown me had been tri-fled with and mislaid, and his armies had also vanished, and everything had fallen through, like my toy trains that, in the winter of 1904–1905, in Wiesbaden, I tried to run over the frozen puddles in the grounds of the Hotel Oranian.

Nabokov ends the section, writing: "The following of such thematic designs through one's life should be, I think, the true purpose of autobiography." A bombshell assertion so calmly offered.

What a Dickensian meeting that must have been! And the juxtaposition of the meeting with the outwardly minor childhood incident is reinforced—brought almost to ironic hyperbole—by his writing "and his armies had also vanished." This is where we see Nabokov's boldness—not in any outsized or distorted presentation, but in his deliberate use of the vastly understating "also" as a connective between the long-lost matches and the vanished armies.

This way of zooming in on one detail—to the exclusion of ostensibly important material—creates the impression of the writer's inner life. It also creates a completely skewed picture of history, one which makes no pretense to being objective. Freed up in this way, Nabokov can let whole years pass unremarked while paragraphs are devoted to the particular marking on the wings of a moth. Immersed as I am in his language—his world—I come to accept his peculiar mode of self-presentation. But there is also a definite arrogance announcing itself.

As subjectively distorted and deliberately understated as Nabokov's version of history might be, however, certain major events do need to be factored in, for their outcomes exerted a profound influence on Nabokov's life trajectory. The spots on the moth's wing are finally *not* as important as the abdication of Tsar Nicholas in 1917, and all that followed from that. Nabokov trusted that his educated readers would automatically fill in the missing matter, as I'm sure most of them did. But I do wonder whether, as the early twentieth century recedes, there won't be a growing number of readers who won't really know the counterpoint narrative. To them, Nabokov's recounting of experience will seem very different from my version, as mine is certainly different from that of readers living in the twenties, thirties, or forties. While Nabokov's subjective presentation remains a kind of constant for every reader, past and future, the understanding of big-picture history and its effects will surely differ from generation to generation.

Other effects and consequences follow from this way of collapsing and excising events. The reader's understanding of Nabokov's family is entirely shaped by the author's decisions about what to include and what not. Nabokov certainly recognized the infinite possibilities of writing his experience, and he surely knew that offering his reader the usual personal account—this following that in a normally scaled narrative—would be a kind of metaphysical perjury. Remember, the title of the first version of the memoir was *Conclusive Evidence*, which I can only read as the writer's sly contradicting wink, for where the self is concerned there is finally no such thing.

I have proposed that Nabokov's decision to be reticent was in order to safeguard privacy. He was writing decades before the tell-all barriers were broken. Rules of decorum, especially among the upper classes, were strict in a way we can scarcely imagine. But also, Nabokov very likely wanted to create the impression of a large well-to-do household—an estate—in which emotional connection is not so easily come by. His overall portrait of his father certainly suggests that kind of scenario. Vladimir Dmitrievich Nabokov was a busy journalist as well as a prominent progressive statesman—we don't ever get to see him as a father.

With Nabokov's mother, as I noted, it's the reverse. I always think of one passage—quite similar to the opening of

Proust's *Remembrance of Things Past,* where Proust's Marcel desperately waits for his mother to come upstairs and kiss him before he goes to sleep. Nabokov, just a young boy, acts out an elaborate dawdling game as he follows his mother up the stairs. "I was merely playing for time by extending every second to its utmost," he explains—until the inevitable moment when she passed him along to his nanny. The emotional longing is palpable. And as we know from other scenes, it is gratified.

As for the siblings—was it that there was just not enough room? Brother Sergei gets a few moments on the stage, but he never comes to life for us. Younger siblings get none at all. This is another thing to consider about scene selection that represents a real controlling power: the memoirist can simply refuse to animate certain people in his story, less from protective impulse, and more like what comes across as a kind of emotional banishment.

It's always interesting to find out how members of one's family react to their portrayal in memoir. When my memoir came out years ago, I was completely blindsided by the responses of some of the people who figured in it. This was my naivete. My father was far more upset than I had expected by the way I had characterized our relationship during my teens and early twenties. My siblings made it clear they were not happy about the short shrift they thought they were given. My old girlfriend was not happy—she let me know specifically that she hated the name I had given her.

Now that I've seen more of the way of things, I

understand these reactions. Harder to grasp is that I would have been surprised at what they had to say. But in all truth, while I was immersed in the writing, I was living in a completely solipsistic world. I was not just looking back on events and people, I was at the same time *creating* them—creating them, I now see, to fit the larger life portrait I was trying to fashion. There were all those central things to consider—what to pay attention to, where to confer importance, what to put in and what to leave out. The choices fell to me. Reading my words, however, people encountered themselves from the outside in an alien light. How could they not feel miscast and slighted?

•

The intersection in memoir of "real life" and representation raises a big question. Simply: what is the relation between the words on the page and the life they look to represent? Tenuous at best, I think. Memoir, as many have said, should be filed in the fiction section of the bookstore. If ever there were such a thing as an unreliable narrator, it is the memoirist. Every remembered moment, every characterization of a person, every suggestion of causality—*everything* is staged. And therefore everything is completely suspect. If we could somehow set the written account alongside the actuality, we would see right away that even the most carefully proportioned memoir is a deliberated "version," in some way most likely the expression of a self that is begging for love and admiration.

As Czeslaw Milosz once quipped: "When a writer is born into a family, the family is finished." That may be an exaggeration, but we do need to ask whether every memoir is, in however veiled a way, an attempted settling of scores with others—or just with life. The writer does not have to argue a case. She has only to say "and this is how it really was." *Was it?* It is a fundamental truth that no one writes or pursues any art out of a life of gratified longing.

How do we sort it all out? If we assume from the start that any given memoir does not in an objective way represent the life, sometimes not even at a stretch, how do we explain why we read? I would answer that we actually read to experience interpretive self-portraiture—which in turn itself needs to be interpreted. We should approach a memoir not as a verifiable account but as a projection of the memoirist's *I*. The reader should attend that *I* in much the same way that the therapist attends the client's narrative. We have to listen to what is being said, but also, on the basis of that, heed closely the unintended "tells." No one gives it straight—"straight" is impossible. Certainly it was for Nabokov. I give no credence at all to our memoirist when he announces, almost proudly, that he remembers almost nothing of his years at Cambridge. Or, obviously, when he mentions his parents' deaths in such a deliberately distanced way.

So, again, why read? The question is obviously rhetorical—there are all kinds of reasons. One of these is an interest in the dynamics of self-revelation—especially in the friction between the writer's presentation and what can be called the received public version of the person. Another reason might involve a fascination with the stylistic feints and tricks: the very things that distort what might be a truer account. I'm thinking here of Nabokov's particular way of rendering the passage of time, the leaps and slow dilations, and also the way he portrays the relation of himself to others.

I know, too, that I'm deeply interested in tracking the author's rendering of the psychological process of coming of age. The effect of reading a memoir might be in some cases likened to that of watching a time-lapse video clip of a butterfly maturing from larva to pupa to adult. In fact, I have little doubt that our obsessed lepidopterist contemplated some way of using such transformation as a structural template.

Above all else, I read an author's memoir to keep company with a person I am interested in. In this one key respect, factual accuracy might not necessarily be that important. For whatever distortions we may come across, we understand that they are in some way reflections of the author—they are another way of getting access to the imagination at work. The words and details are the author's, and we can grant them the same importance we grant those we find in the work.

The Soul Inside the Sentence

WRITERS USE DETAILS TO INTENSIFY the reader's immersion in the narrative. Not just any details, of course, but the ones that compel attention and through their unexpectedness provoke fresh seeing. These are not the kinds of details that we find in genre prose, which is to say generic prose—the sun "sparkling" on the lake, the gate "creaking" open . . . They are, rather, the details a serious writer discovers by going back deep into her material. When they turn up in the prose, they feel like "finds," unexpected things that somehow confirm that the writer has moved some distance into the inner unknown.

Nabokov has sometimes been characterized by critics as a kind of magician. Michael Wood, one of the writer's most astute interpreters, titles his book on Nabokov *The Magician's Doubts*. I like that designation. It suggests consummate precision and the use of subtle feints, as well as an existential unease about the whole enterprise. For me, no question, Nabokov's magic begins in the sentence and continues from there. More than with most other writers, I will pause in my reading and think, "How in the world did he just do that?"

Nabokov has his own practiced ways of producing illusion. One way to get closer to his specific sleights of hand is to look at the sentences—which, we might remember, he wrote out, one at a time, on index cards, which he then arranged into sequences.

•

Like many others, I first came to Nabokov through reading *Lolita* and, also like many others, I was hooked by the time I reached the bottom of page one. "Lo-lee-ta," etc. The language had seduced me long before I got engaged with the plot. Nabokov's style was arch, morose, and quick across the synapses. Reading prose like this always brings me right up against the fundamental mystery of literature—how it is that the right words, the right word sounds, and the right cadence can combine together and create life on the page? Nabokov is a consummate practitioner of these dark arts. With syntax and diction and who knows what else, he is able to evoke what William Gass called "the soul inside the sentence." I feel it as I read, but I can't begin to explain how this alchemy happens.

A sentence is a string of words arranged according to certain syntactical rules. The rules may be finite, but the possible cumulative outcomes are infinite. It's like chess in this one way. Just as no two writers share the same subjective worldview, so no two accounts of anything will ever be exactly the same. For it's a given that the writer's personality, or inwardness, will impinge on the choice and arrangement of words. My phrasing here is a stiff way of speaking about a matter that is finally very intimate.

Many writers produce excellent prose, no question, and many are rewarded for that. But there is a difference between that excellence and the extra quality—the X factor—that breaks what might be called the fourth wall of the page and achieves a compelling inner animation.

What do I mean? I'll start with an example from Chapter 5, where Nabokov immerses in memory and brings to life Mademoiselle O, one of the several governesses he had when he was growing up. The scene has the ample Mademoiselle getting into a sleigh. He describes her climbing in, clutching the helper out of fear that the sleigh will start moving before she has settled, and finally seating herself with a grunt:

At the juicy smack of their driver's lips the two black horses, Zoyka and Zinka, strain their quarters, shift hooves, strain again; and then Mademoiselle gives a backward jerk of her torso as the heavy sleigh is wrenched out of its world of steel, fur, flesh, to enter a frictionless medium where it skims along a spectral road that it seems barely to touch.

I had to double-check at this point that the memoir was not translated but was written originally in English. It was. I did this because I refused to believe that the cadences, word-sounds, and complexities of sentence-work could have been managed by a translator—unless, of course, that translator happened to be Nabokov himself.

Nabokov's method of working sentence by sentence on separate cards might be relevant here. The practice is about more than just a preferred paper size. The real question is: what kind of mind prefers to create away from the open field of a white page? A page is like a moving horizon; it is implicitly about forward movement, a progress from top to bottom that is renewed again and again. But this customary mode does not apply to Nabokov. He works, instead, like a jeweler with his loupe, like a lepidopterist. Indeed, writing a sentence on a card can be compared to bearing down on some small winged thing with the artificially constrained and intensified focus that a magnifying glass allows.

I would first characterize the whole of that sentence. This is nothing if not an action-centered moment. Consider just the verbs: *smack, strain, shift, strain, gives, is wrenched, enter, skims* . . . Looking at these verbs alone, we can feel the main dynamic of the sequence. It moves from a struggle with obstacles to a sudden liberation as *wrenched* yields to *enter* and *skims*. The verbs support a transfer of focus from the *driver's lips* to *the two black horses* to Mademoiselle's *torso* to *sleigh* and finally to the *road*—which the sleigh is seen to barely touch.

A sentence like this was probably not dashed off in a single sweep of inspiration. Most likely, it was constructed, calculated—not in any mechanical sense, but in the sense of emerging from an artisan's considered craft. Looking from this perspective, using index cards has a certain psychological logic. Nabokov's approach short-circuits the writer's usual forward impetus and emphasizes the singularity of every unit. The marvel, to me, is that though he works in increments like this, the result does not at all feel like a collage. The writer does not sacrifice a natural narrative motion.

There are a few more things to be said about this example. For one thing, it's a species of sentence that belongs to an earlier time, what was once referred to as the "periodic sentence"—that is, a sentence that is not complete before the final word, or phrase, has been put in place. This sentence about Mademoiselle is a perfect example. It requires the closing phrase, the skimming along the "spectral road," to create its effect. The move toward closure is what helps to generate the propulsion. One feature of the periodic sentence, seen in this example, is that it creates suspense, pulling the reader ahead with the anticipation of completion—the "other shoe" effect. Fewer and fewer contemporary writers resort to such sentences, for they do carry a feel of being constructed. Which they are. Nabokov's syntax here (and so often elsewhere) is deliberately torqued. But it needs to be torqued to convey the intended effect—first of exertion and difficulty, and then of swiftness and lightness. To me, the sensory effect feels worth the labor that produced it.

Staying with the sentence, I also note the close-focus accuracy of word choice and the subtle manipulations of

Nabokov's syntax. The first we see in the interplay of verbs and nouns. I am reminded of Flaubert's famous search for the right words and with that, naturally, the best way of combining them. This requires more than just a verbal finesse. The right words do not arrive out of thin air, or the dictionary. They come when the author has not merely imagined, but in some sense also re-experienced in himself the sensations depicted. It is the matching of sensation or observation to the words that is the secret. Without that exacting equivalence, when words are chosen largely for display, the result is quite different.

To this point, I was looking up something about *Speak, Memory*, when I came across John Updike's praise for the memoir: "Nabokov has never written English better than in these reminiscences," he writes, "never has he written so sweetly . . . With tender precision and copious wit . . . inspired by an atheist's faith in the magic of simile and the sacredness of lost time, Nabokov makes of his past a brilliant icon—bejewelled, perspectiveless, untouchable."

Updike was known as a "mandarin"—ornate—stylist. And right here, ironically, I find an illustrative counter-example to Nabokov's mode. Updike creates a smooth and melodic groove for his praises, but then, in praising, he shows us how easy it is to slide into a mode of inflated baroque. He is all modifiers—*tender precision, copious wit, atheist's faith, magic of simile, sacredness of lost time, brilliant icon, bejeweled, perspectiveless, untouchable*—and when you peel those away, you cannot determine what it is he is really praising.

The word for all these variations of verbal construction is, of course, style. How a writer makes a sentence obviously reveals a certain amount, but style is most easily recognized over a progression of sentences. Reading a paragraph, a page, a chapter, we pick up all sorts of subliminal clues that a sentence, however characteristic, can't necessarily provide. A longer section of prose reveals rhythms, and rhythms suggest not only thought patterns, but also intensities of emotional pitch. They reveal character. The old gendered pronouncement "the style is the man " is variously attributed and has an extended historical pedigree. It is founded on an assumption of psychological as well as physical equivalences. A person of melancholic temperament, for example, is not likely to express herself in short declarative sentences. Proust, the ailing cork-lined room *isolato,* felt no qualms about weaving paragraph-long verbal brocades. Raymond Carver gathers short flat sentences into larger suggestive scenarios. And Beckett, meanwhile, mutters dour and darkly comic asides.

How do we read Nabokov's voice on the page? I have to pause here to collect my adjectives. He is sardonic, playful, melancholic, fanatically precise, and many other things besides. Whatever his mode—or mood—he is able to convey that very rare sensation of awakened life, and doing so he confirms for me that the nature, or atmosphere, of a word, any word, changes according to context, how it interacts with other words. Under the best conditions, words together are no longer just designations—entities that a dictionary can encompass—they are elements that can change their nature to create a specific current. Which is the end to which a great writer uses them.

Thinking in this way about style, and the idea that a writer's personality and character impinge on everything he writes, I would further suggest that the writer's character is also a kind of ground—an existential foundation. It's interesting. Clever or playful as Nabokov can be, the reader nevertheless understands that those notes sound against a profound sense of loss, a pervasive nostalgia. It is the difference between, say, a sociable individual smiling and another—the survivor of some traumatic event, say—making the same facial expression. I believe we can tell the difference, even if we can't quite say why. When we read, we also *read*—interpret—and our sense of that second person's emotional condition naturally deepens when we realize that such a smile might take an effort.

This may explain why as a reader I give Nabokov's instances of cleverness a weight that I don't give to most other writers. For me it's a case of *smile, though your heart is breaking . . .*

Nabokov writes about his loss of home so poignantly in *Speak Memory*, that we carry it as an underlying context throughout. Though his tone is mainly lyrical, it reaches an intensified saturation when he addresses the idea of the gone past directly :

A sense of security, of well-being, of summer warmth pervades my memory. That robust reality makes a ghost of the present. The mirror brims with brightness; a bumblebee has entered the room and bumps against the ceiling. Everything is as it should be, nothing will ever change, nobody will ever die.

The passage, to me, is so compelling because of that third sentence, the proliferating *b*-sound that lets us feel the motion of the bumblebee inside the room. The single *b* of bumps could not convey the sensation by itself. The nostalgia is amplified by the next sentence, which is so abstract after the previous one. And the ephemerality of all things is underscored by Nabokov's insistence on that blatant reversal of what he know is the truth. For a split-second we, too, believe it—nothing will ever change—but only for that long.

Metaphor

WE WON'T GET FAR EXAMINING Nabokov's prose style without paying attention to his use of metaphor. Metaphor is the great variable, working like yeast inside the sentence, the mysterious agency of transformation and sometimes a whirling sort of liftoff. Metaphor is favored by poets because, properly used, it can bring a sudden amplitude into the close quarters of a stanza. Maybe this is what Joseph Brodsky meant when he quipped: "Prose is infantry, poetry is air force." Though he is mainly writing prose, Nabokov uses the transforming powers of metaphor for his own purposes. In one instance, he recalls being a young boy traveling on one of those old grand deluxe trains. As he tells it:

> One night, during a trip abroad, in the fall of 1903, I recall kneeling on my (flattish) pillow at the window of a sleeping car (probably on the long-extinct Mediterranean Train de Luxe, the one whose six cars had the lower part of their body

painted in umbers and the panels in cream) and seeing with an inexplicable pang, a handful of fabulous lights that beckoned to me from a distant hillside, and then slipped into a pocket of black velvet: diamonds that I later gave away to my characters to alleviate the burden of my wealth.

Almost everything here depends on metaphor. The first half of the sentence is elaborate in its syntax, but it is literal, without device. Figurative speech takes over only when he remembers seeing a "handful" of lights, a usage so common that we take it in without even noticing. Next, also familiar, are the lights that "beckoned." But then the real transformations begin. The already humanized lights are said to have "slipped into a pocket of black velvet." What Nabokov means, I think, is that the train has entered a tunnel, though the figurative "pocket" is by definition a *cul de sac*. Black velvet carries a suggestion of a jewelry pouch, which eases the way of the next transformation: the lights have now been concretized as diamonds, and the diamonds, having for just a moment materialized, right away dematerialize into conceptual entities to be given away to imagined characters—to "alleviate the burden" of Nabokov's wealth. What he means by "wealth" here is not clear, but the action is a kind of wish, for of course the transfer of anything to created characters does not really alleviate anything.

Here's another set of sentences:

At a collapsible table, my mother and I played a card game called *durachki*. Although it was broad daylight, our cards, a glass and, on a different plane, the locks of a suitcase were reflected in the window. Through forest and field, and in sudden ravines, and among scuttling cottages, those discarnate gamblers kept steadily playing on for sparkling stakes.

Nabokov uses a different sort of metaphor here, making use of one of his favorite strategies, which is to present an action indirectly, via some refraction or distortion. He is once again remembering riding on a train, and, as always, he invites us to carefully attend the details. Doing so, we end up performing an elaborate visual assemblage. First, there is the straight-on introduction: he and his mother are playing cards. From this he moves to the visual reflection, allowing that to convey the next elaboration of the optics. There is a subtle and slightly taxing shift when he notes how the locks on the suitcase are there on another plane—a literal plane (and pane)—which we take a moment to register.

Nabokov's culminating moment comes when we are asked to picture both the scenery shuddering by—forest, field, ravines, and cottages—*and* the card players shimmering transparently on the surface of the glass. The imagery suggests that the players are no longer literal. They have become discarnate and the stakes they play for are "sparkling."

This is obviously a writer who must be read with the

greatest care. Almost any sentence or passage that I chose to linger over as I read turned out to be far subtler than I had thought. I did at times wonder if a certain effect was intended, or was just a happy accident. I find a case in point in the passage I just cited. I zero in on Nabokov's use of the adjective "sudden," which is just the kind of thing a reader is apt to skim right over. But slowing down, attending to that sentence, I find it to be very much the right—and I assume now purposeful—word. For *sudden* has us realizing that the ravines are being crossed laterally, that they are just a flash in the peripheral vision.

Though they are kindred figures of speech used to convey analogy, there is a significant difference between similes and metaphors. In building the bridge of likeness, a simile closes the circuit, as it were. "He stood in the distance like a statue." The direct comparison deepens the impression, as it is meant to—"statue" conveys complete immobility and apartness—but it does not widen out much further. Whereas "he was a statue in the distance" leaves behind a subtle trace of mystery. Though we know it is merely likeness that is suggested, the direct transformation of person to thing is more forceful, and not completely resolved. For there to be resolution he would have to be transformed back. "He was a statue in the distance, but then the statue suddenly shifted and we saw that it was our friend."

Nabokov, as we observe throughout, is a master at creating these liminal effects—one thing becoming another, boundaries shifting. He is no surrealist, though. He stays just within the bounds of the real, but his "real" always has a mysterious vibration, a feeling of being something more than appearances indicate.

VISUAL TRICKS

If there is one particular effect which Nabokov "owns," it's his way of creating a scene or describing a thing by way of distortion. I don't mean any kind of bending of appearances, but, rather, a natural—literal—transcription of what is seen. The only departure from the norm is that the thing, or scene, is viewed through a prism, or by way of some reflecting surface, or a lens. Earlier passages I've quoted have made some use of this, but it is significant—and recurrent—enough to be examined as an actual strategy.

I already cited the scene of Nabokov playing cards with his mother, in which uses a series of optical distortions to give an impressionistic, but also almost cubist rendition of the experience. Paging through, I find another such train episode. Trains, for whatever reason, seem to prompt Nabokov to use his various "special" effects, so many of them making use of some calculated visual distortion. In this case, he does not make use of lenses or reflections, but he does use the window views, along with a rhythmic sense of the train's momentum, to simulate his own state of vertigo:

> I would keep catching the car in the act of being recklessly sheathed, lurching waiters and all, in the landscape, while the landscape itself went through

a complex system of motion, the daytime moon keeping stubbornly abreast of one's plate, the distant meadows opening fanwise, the near trees sweeping up on invisible swings toward the track, a parallel rail line all at once committing suicide by anastomosis, a bank of nictitating grass rising, rising, rising, until the little witness of mixed velocities was made to disgorge his portion of *omelette aux confitures de fraises.*

Nabokov so often writes these highly complicated passages in a playful way. He is, of course, showing off— lining up his separate details, arranging them into a sequence, and then choreographing his syntax for maximum impact. In this case, he is again making use of the periodic sentence, that delaying stagger that only delivers the intended impact at the very end. We can feel the spring tightening as we read. First, there is the dizzying burlesque of waiters with full trays lurching past each other in the aisle of the dining car. This leads via easy transition to awareness of the landscape outside the windows, offered up with all of those gratifyingly exact bits: the meadows opening "fanwise," the trees seeming to swing up, the odd deflecting phrasing of "suicide by anastomosis" [a crossing of various parts of a network] and "nictitating" [suggesting a whitish membrane] grass, leading to the repeated "rising, rising, rising" and at last to the decorously offered image of young Nabokov abruptly throwing up the omelette he had just eaten.

Like many mandarin stylists, Nabokov takes pleasure in a certain verbal obscurantism: *anastomosis* and *nictitating* being the most immediate examples. Use of these "dictionary" words naturally—and deliberately—signals linguistic snobbism. No one would ever exonerate Nabokov from *that*. Users of such pedantic locutions are precision fiends by temperament. We will see that the same obsession with accuracy and detail is found as well in his lepidopterist's taxonomic fetishism as well as his interest in working through highly complicated chess moves.

Nabokov's arcane usages naturally reflect the author's temperament, but I also think that they are placed there by design in order to pull us out of the narration for a moment—to remind us that we are dealing with a linguistic artifact, a worked-over construction, as opposed to a more hospitable and casual sort of expression. The man, we know, is a formalist, a writer who never gives in to a more relaxed position. Just as he carefully pincered his sentences together on index cards, he also insisted on conducting interviews by mail, receiving questions and then answering them in a considered—and crafted—way.

Nabokov's fascination with optical devices that alter one's perception started at a very early age. Near the beginning of the memoir, he elaborates on one of his boyhood fascinations with a toy he played with during a family stay on the Riviera: "a meerschaum penholder with a tiny peephole of crystal in its ornamental part." Put to the eye, though, this curious little trinket suddenly offers "a miraculous photographic view of the bay and line of cliffs ending in a lighthouse that could be seen inside."

The man loves the various devices that force us to see the world from a different vantage, like this contrived miniaturization that captures and shrinks some part of a scene and renders it as a tableaux. Why does he do this? Why does he give us these observations in great detail—but obliquely, by way of some distortion? I don't think it's just for the pleasure of the trick—though there is that. His deeper intent might also have to do with the strange differential between seeing something directly and seeing its transformed aspect. Looking at the latter can have the effect of sharpening the focus on the real thing. Or else, maybe the tension between the two images somehow confirms that everything we behold is only a version. In fact, we might even consider that the artifice of the prose is itself another version. Could he be including the meerschaum penholder satirically, as a statement on the writer's verbal construction of the world? Is the verbal artifact any more "real" than what the gimmick shows? Nabokov—the magician—would surely have considered these distinctions.

Another passage gives us further insight into this stylistic move. In this case, Nabokov gives us a scene—once again lightly mocking in tone—in which one of his boyhood tutors has arranged an evening event at the estate. The presentation will feature the projection of image-transparencies on a makeshift screen. It is the early 1900s, so any projected image is a novelty. This set-up is, naturally, a perfect occasion for Nabokov to make use of some of his favorite sleights of hand.

"Now that I come to think of it," he writes, remembering, "how tawdry and tumid they looked, those jellylike pictures projected upon the damp linen screen" but then adds,

> what loveliness the glass slides as such revealed when simply held between finger and thumb and raised to the light—translucent miniatures, pocket wonderlands, neat little worlds of hushed luminous hues! In later years, I rediscovered the same precise and silent beauty at the radiant bottom of a microscope's magic shaft.

Looking at the slide of the reduced specimen, he finds a different transformation, one that also compels his fancy: the tiny insect is suddenly rendered large, available for calm inspection. "There is," he writes, "in the dimensional scale of the world a kind of delicate meeting place between imagination and knowledge, a point arrived at by diminishing large things and enlarging small ones, that is intrinsically artistic."

How interesting: this idea of altered scales providing a "delicate meeting place between imagination and knowledge"—which, in Nabokov's view, is "intrinsically artistic." He is making a suggestive observation, no question, but what does it mean? How is it that imagination and knowledge come together? One way might be that by creating a gap or dissonance between what we assume to be the right scale of a thing and its magnification or diminution, the writer invites us to engage the image, translating the seen thing back to familiar scale, and at the same time to experience the estrangement. Estrangement, which his countryman, the critic Viktor Shklovsky, took to be the key to "seeing." The viewer is confronted with the unexpected version of a thing and thereby stripped of her customary contexts. Her engagement with the anomaly calls on the imagination, creates around it a new context, trying to make it fit. This is, on a different level, what draws children to model trains or doll houses. Their intricate minimizations create an alternatively scaled world, one that invites a focused projection of fantasy.

These adjustments by the imagination underlie many of Nabokov's optical distortions. Depicting the locks of a suitcase reflected in the window forces on us the double-take, the momentary catch that involves an act of visual interpretation. We are all but directed to put the lock back in its rightful place overhead. The momentary estrangement has sharpened things for us; it has given us the pleasure of getting it right.

The manipulation of proportions and distortions of the expected is a contrarian move meant to refresh our seeing. It is of a piece with Nabokov's approach to his entire memoir, where he repeatedly foregrounds the immediate perception and leaves the larger familial or historical context as a background blur. He invites us in close but keeps us at a distance from other perspectives. The effect of this, whether intended or not, is to induce in the reader a certain sensory disorder, a synesthesia-like melding of perceptions and expectations.

•

Are these recurring manipulations the product of Nabokov's intention or his disposition? I ask this thinking of his life-long obsession with butterflies, an obsession that demands the keenest eye for detail—this tiny spot on a wing, that striation, that camouflaging capacity. Nabokov admits at one point to being fascinated by nature's mechanisms of adaptation, how a coloration of a certain species evolved to match the local flora; how a butterfly could convincingly become a scrap of bark on a tree. The facts of the matter are science, yes, but science here starts to shade into something else. Nabokov's focus on the uncanny evokes poetic simile—the moth is like the tree's bark—which leads us back into the poet's realm. Though he is focused on the tiniest objective details, Nabokov surely saw them as further confirmation of a larger mystery.

Thinking about Nabokov's fixation on butterflies, I am reminded of Walter Benjamin's observation about collecting —that "every obsession borders on chaos." I have wondered for years about what he meant by that, but pondering it now, I begin to see. To say an obsession borders on chaos is to identify it as a resistance, a fire wall, a kind of coping mechanism that proposes that the intense focus on anything can be a shield against psychological turmoil. But obsession is not a distraction, a diversion of the mind—it is a full engagement of our being. The engagement replaces one focus with another, but it also allows a transfer of energies that is a new kind of interpretation.

It's true that Nabokov discovered his passion for butterflies long before war and exile changed everything in his life. But the chaotic events that followed—which are held at such a remove in *Speak, Memory*—apparently only intensified his mania for chasing, mounting, sorting and organizing. Collecting is, of course, all about creating order, searching for completion. An analogous defense against chaos the distancing is maintained by crafted prose and an intense bearing down on immediate perceptions.

Of course, that displacement cannot keep everything at bay. The underlying feeling of the memoir—but really of any of Nabokov's works—is, for me, a deep and defended sadness. In everything he writes, he seems to be saying that this kind of expression, this art, is as far as recovery and redemption can go. The past is a *fata morgana*. It shimmers there, almost within reach, but is ultimately not to be had.

Family Photos

MY COPY OF *SPEAK, MEMORY*, by now a fairly battered old hardcover, has fifteen separate photos which are clustered at intervals throughout the book. Not in any sense artistic, the images are black-and-white, family-album quality: posed group pictures, grainy headshots of individuals, mostly members of Nabokov's family and relatives. I wonder about the decision to include them and position them in this way.

Their presence in the memoir—they can hardly be ignored—unsettles me, not because of their contents, but because they are there. When I stop to study any one of them, I feel the clash between categories. It's as if I were reading a novel and suddenly came upon an insert with images of the main characters. To my mind, a work like Nabokov's is closer to a novel than a biography, if only by virtue of the literary prose and the scenic approach. Looking at "real world" images, I'm not sure how to react. Either I can absorb the dissonance and move on, or I can project the mood of the prose onto the photos. With *Speak Memory,* I have tried to read into them, hoping to make them part of my experience. But I've never really succeeded.

This is not to say that the photos do not fascinate me—they do. But they inevitably point me toward the outward verifiable life, to the continuum that is so-called history, whereas the prose pulls me to Nabokov's lyric subjectivity and the relativity of events processed and ordered by memory.

I do also experience a personal reaction apart from all literary considerations. As I wrote earlier, parts of my own family history overlapped some of these same times and places. Though I have no Russian blood, and though my family was not of the Nabokovs' social class, both my father's parents spent some time in Russia. My grandfather was, as mentioned, a liberal anti-Czar activist, my grandmother a student. I have an old sepia-tinged photo from that time, taken a few years before the revolution, that shows them sitting at an outdoor table in Smolensk with a group of their fellow liberals. It could find its place right beside any one of the photos from that era in this book.

I recognize another, more general visual kinship. Many of the family photos I have from that era—posed portraits, images of city streets and country retreats—are in the same key, part of the same Zeitgeist as those in the memoir. Clothes, postures, expressions—you would think that people had not yet learned to smile. When I come upon any of the photographs in the memoir, therefore, I register much more than the surface content. I feel both a documentary and sentimental connection. I can't not imbue the Nabokov photos with some of the sentiments I have about those showing my family's own past.

Contemplating the images, I want to break through the surface, to get myself back into a time and a place. It's a kind of imaginative projection that I practice all the time with photographs of family members or old friends—I can't *not*. I suppose it's my way of trying to get closer to certain sensations of time. How can it be that X was alive so long ago and looked like that? Or: how is the face I recognize from years ago related to the face I saw last week? What was the world like then, how did it feel to be in that time? They are all vague, elusive questions, but I can't deny that they work on me.

The photography question thus becomes part of the metaphysical terrain of memoir. Where a memoirist like Nabokov is relentless in the effort to get back, using the pressure of language to reanimate bygones, the photographer is looking at the moment and not giving posterity any thought. Years later, paradoxically, the deepening powers of time invest the image—any image—with an unintended potency. The poignancy of Nabokov's family photos—like that of most old photographs—comes from the subjects' innocence of what the future will bring, which duplicates our own innocence about the same thing.

The Muse Visits

IT DOES SEEM ALMOST SCRIPTED by Freud—that when Nabokov, still in his teens, finished his first poem, he rushed to read it to his mother. The scene, touched on earlier, is one of the most memorably intimate scenes in the memoir.

I don't know that this is exactly a case of "mother as muse"—there was after all a young woman, an implied addressee, in the picture—but there is no question that the fifteen-year-old poet was desperate to get his mother's approval. Which he got most gratifyingly—tears streaming—and I would theorize that for him inspiration and love were from that point on entwined at the root.

Still, given that writing was the central thing in Nabokov's life, I'm surprised that he finally devotes only one short chapter to his very first effort, and basically nothing more. No less surprising is that he writes that chapter in a way that in places reads like a hyperbolic send-up of creative inspiration. The chapter is as much about the romantic self-aggrandizement of youth as it is about the poem. I think of Keats' "Oh what can ail Thee, knight at arms/alone and palely loitering?"

Nabokov's inspiration comes to him in an old wooden pavilion on the family estate—he is on his way home from seeing his latest true love, when a rainstorm suddenly breaks. The intensity of nature is conducive to inspiration and the writer works especially hard to create the setting and atmosphere. Young Nabokov in the pavilion is all attention. To the point where he even notes a "dead horsefly . . . on its back near the brown remains of a birch ament."

I start to raise my hand to object—no one goes back some forty years and retrieves such a detail—but then I catch myself and think: why not? Nabokov's moment of observation does directly precede the arrival of the Muse. His senses are very likely fired up. If I pause to consider certain specific—frozen—memories of my own, I have to concede that any number of "insignificant" details remain vivid. Nabokov might very well have preserved the moment. He is, after all, the arch-rememberer, and the burst of first inspiration is like the striking bolt of first love: about some things we remember everything.

As Nabokov writes the scene, the inspiration is somehow infused with the sudden fury of the storm and its equally sudden cessation:

> The rain, which had been a mass of violently descending water wherein the trees writhed and rolled, was reduced all at once to oblique lines of silent gold

breaking into short and long dashes against a background of subsiding vegetable agitation.

Once again we see the effectiveness of his sequence of verbs: *writhed* and *rolled, breaking, subsiding.* The calm arrives mid-sentence. And with the calm, this:

A moment later my first poem began. What touched it off? I think I know. Without any wind blowing, the sheer weight of a raindrop, shining in parasitic luxury on a cordate leaf, caused its tip to dip, and what looked like a globule of quicksilver performed a sudden glissando down the center vein, and then, having shed its bright load, the relieved leaf unbent.

I find the prose here too rich for my taste, but there is no denying the craft, how Nabokov creates tension, building suspense through slow-moving descriptive phrases, and then—this is another beautifully realized periodic sentence—lets the very last word give release: the "relieved leaf" unbends.

He remarks that extended moment as a "fissure" in time, a "missed heartbeat," and then follows up to say that his held-breath suspension "was refunded at once by a patter of rhymes," which he then likens to the patter of rain that comes when a gust of wind blows through the wet trees. The inner (poetry) and outer (rain) are, within the confines of a single sentence, welded together. Such an intensely close observing of the raindrop is surely meant to mark a moment of the purest attention—a powerfully concentrated act of seeing which may have been the triggering event in itself.

While Nabokov speaks of the patter of rain and the sudden arrival of rhymes, he leaves unanswered the question of how the one might have touched off the other. That remains a suggestive analogy—which is finally appropriate. After all, no one has ever explained the workings of inspiration. On this one score Nabokov might actually agree with his nemesis, Freud, who once wrote, with the full frustration of an analyst dealing with an impossible patient: "Before the problem of the creative artist, psychoanalysis must, alas, lay down its arms."

The tension of the droplet suggests the intensity of the moment and serves as a lead-up to what follows. For with the arrival of the inspiration—that inexplicable impulse—he shows himself as entering a prolonged trance, a state which he describes as a completely removed absorption. "I might be wandering at one moment in the depths of the park," he writes, "and the next be pacing the rooms of the house."

He is promoting a somewhat exaggerated picture of the inspiration state. But, to be fair, there do exist accounts in literary history of various striking visitations. Many are drug-assisted (Coleridge writing *Kublai Khan*; Kerouac, on benzedrine, hammering out *On the Road* in one extended bender). But there are also other, presumably *un*assisted, flights—García Márquez being overcome while driving by the sudden and irresistible impulse to begin what would become *One Hundred Years of Solitude*—which he then wrote in one obsessed period. Or the unexpected rush of words and images that led to Rilke to compose of *The Duino Elegies* over a period of days . . . Yet while each of these writers has testified to being caught up in a creative surge, I don't know that anyone has romanticized the state of possession quite like the fifteen-year-old Nabokov has. His perception of the leaf and raindrop says a great deal.

Judging from the artful transitions he makes in the course of his creative rapture, here and there making note of those briefest moments of contact with his normal life, Nabokov is having some sport, playing the daily and timeless states off against each other. But then again, he might be using this one dramatic instance to represent the various visitations of the Muse that he must have experienced over a long writing life.

But this, too, becomes a tricky conjecture. Because Nabokov has, we know, described his mode of composition—proceeding sentence by sentence on separate index cards. The pressure of such applied craft shows us a much more deliberative artist. It would seem that he made the transition from inspiration to discipline, which finally served him very well.

Chapter eleven is really the only part of the memoir in which Nabokov deals with writing, his lifelong passion. His restraint on the subject could be another instance of maintaining privacy. But he might also, in a sense, be heeding Wittgenstein's well-known precept: that whatever we cannot explain we must pass over in silence. And really, how can a writer, the sole participant in this charged process, describe it in any way that does it justice? The sparks of association leap so quickly that there is no real possibility of capturing them. And the mysterious transitions, how ideas and intuitions find the right words—who can account for those? I've never found a convincing psychological explanation. This too might partly explain why accounts of the *how* of composition are so rare.

One key to the creative act—and so many artists have testified to this—is the shift from fragmented ordinary time to duration. For the creator in the throes of composition, the clock seems to stop. Nabokov is clearly tantalized—as we see in this scene and throughout his work—by occasions when all awareness of time disappears. Here the transitions from one state to the other are of special interest. There is the going away from the clock, and then the disorienting return. T.S. Eliot characterized the moment beautifully when he wrote "you are the music as long as the music lasts."

But where does the writer *go*? What happens? When Nabokov writes of fissures and gaps in time, he is getting at this strangely suspended condition. Duration is a liberation, an escape into a state free of the ticking clock and unvexed by our usual distraction or else the moment-to-moment awareness of everything around us. It is the time of contemplation, open to the unconscious. The deepest art comes out of duration, and I believe it retains some of that aura of timelessness. This is something that the reader, viewer, and listener can partake in when they are paying full attention to the work in question.

The Collector

MANY PEOPLE HAVE TWO BASIC associations with Nabokov. He is either the author of *Lolita*, with its formerly titillating and now—societally speaking—full-out aura of taboo, or else the eccentric butterfly collector. The author was widely known for stalking these insects across continents. He was serious, and it's true that some of his prize rarities can be found in the Harvard museum collections. But it must be said that there do exist various photographs of a plump elderly man in shorts and knee socks clambering up or down some grassy hillside with a butterfly net in his hand. Nabokov himself, so I remember from somewhere, found these photos comic—in his own famously cantankerous way, of course.

So much about public Nabokov is easy to fit into a biographical description—his years as a professor in America, his happy marriage to Vera, and his proud fatherhood. The obsessive collecting is another matter. As a boy who now and then walked around with a net and captured

Tiger Swallowtails and Monarchs and very little else, I can relate to the early-on pleasures of the chase, as well as the impulse to preserve and mount the captures. But that same passion carried on and intensified in an adult is, for me, less easy to explain.

Lepidoptery was, for Nabokov, a compulsion that he could not quite control—he pretty much admitted it. I've come across any number of written scenes that show Nabokov or one of his fictional characters in the midst of some important moment—a conversation, a kiss—suddenly spying some bit of flutter out of the corner of the eye and losing all sense of the matter at hand. The collector is possessed, ever alert. Butterflies are not only a consuming hobby—they are also an expression of a deeply rooted psychological fixation.

This leads me back to Walter Benjamin, but now to quote the full sentence. "Every passion borders on chaos," he writes, adding "that of the collector borders on the chaos of memory." A tantalizing but elusive assertion. For starters, what is the relation of passion to chaos? The suggestion is that true passion is ungovernable, that the will has been taken over, subverted. Moreover, there is a possibility that such an intensity of feeling is liable to flee all bounds. We have impulse as opposed to logic, chaos against order.

But how does collecting have anything to do with memory, and how is memory a "chaos"? I don't think I can parse this out completely. With Nabokov, my thinking veers into basic psychology: that his childhood passion became a fixation after the trauma of war and exile. That collecting at that point stopped being a hobby and became a stay against inner disruption. While the former life was lost and the new life was uncertain, butterflies were still butterflies. Chasing and collecting them in whatever country brought a kind of stability—they could be netted, pinned, classified, inserted into a highly orderly system.

But Benjamin, looking to find the origin, or cause, of the collector's compulsion, here brings memory into the equation. Nabokov's experience changed his collecting from a childhood sport to a symbolically-charged effort of restoration. Collectors, as we know, often fetishize objects that relate to their childhood, whether those are baseball cards, dolls, or other particular kinds of memorabilia. By collecting, they perpetuate an emotional link. In this way, the butterflies might have come to represent a core aspect of the childhood that Nabokov strove to retrieve—the writing of the memoir and the collecting pursuit might share a link, if not a common point of origin.

Collecting is not just about acquisition—the collector acquires with the hope of achieving a totality. There is the premise that the completion of a set brings some kind of closure. But does it ever? Possibly it does with baseball cards, but with butterflies there can never be any real completion. The desire for totality is repeatedly mocked by the erratic fluttering that is so often just out of reach. The collector is goaded on—might this be an unclassified new species?

Freud had an idea that he called *fort-da*, which some

have argued is the primal basis of all narrative. I love the simplicity as well as the obvious truth of it. A child throws its toy from the crib—*Fort*—and then, bereft, cries for its return: *Da*. We are all at some level governed by loss and the desire for restitution, as we are by another Freudian pair— *eros* and *thanatos*. *Fort-da* can be seen to account for much in the Nabokovian universe. The problem is that loss is one thing and compensation another. How much can a beautifully realized work prompted by loss redeem that loss?

Nabokov's obsession with butterflies far surpassed his interest in chess problems. Because lepidoptery is about much more than just gathering. It is also about collating specimens based on distinctions and variations, often very subtle ones, and was in that way perfectly suited to his punctiliousness about detail. In his *Lectures on Literature*, he devotes the opening part of his lecture on Kafka's "The Metamorphosis" by correcting the received idea that Gregor Samsa woke up to find he was a cockroach. It was, argues Nabokov, in fact a specific kind of beetle, and the popular misunderstanding was no small matter. This is how pedants and compulsives see the world. The level of detailing that characterizes his prose is on a par with the details that so fascinate him in the quest for butterflies.

The detail individuates. Or, as historian Aby Warburg declared, "God is in the detail." I've also heard the variant— that it is the Devil who is to be found there.

Butterflies, writing . . . chess. Chess, Nabokov's other passion, springs from a different impulse. If chasing butterflies is outward turning, centrifugal, chess is completely inward. Where most collecting is, at least technically, finite, the possibilities of chess games are infinite, and the operations of mind of the chess player are naturally very different from those of the collector/taxonomist. It's hard not to think of F. Scott Fitzgerald's words in "The Crack Up" : "The test of a first rate intelligence is the ability to hold two opposed ideas in the mind at the same time, and still retain the ability to function."

Collectors, by and large, look back. They recover objects that for them have a strong subjective resonance. Chess players, meanwhile, are always directing themselves toward new combinations. Serious chess players do of course spend time studying the various board situations and classic solutions by the masters of the past, but their play is always about the future—the upcoming move—anticipating and calculating.

The premise of chess—as even a completely ineffectual player like me knows—is anticipating problems and their possible solutions. A good chess player must have an instinct about the opponent, as well as an ability to hold various patterns and projections in his mind. It is a dense and specific meditation.

Of these two compulsive activities, collecting clearly seems more suited to memoir, and chess to fiction. The novelist, too, is forever imagining and factoring forward, whereas the memoirist gathers and arranges, and—necessarily—invents. What the two activities do share is a need for resolute focus—as, of course, does writing. These comparisons are highly simplistic, but they have some basis in practice. Further, we know that different activities call on different energies and aptitudes. That Nabokov excelled in collecting *and* solving chess problems reveals an interesting psychological split. His completely unique prose may have something to do with that split.

"The Old Questions: There's Nothing Like Them."

A FEW YEARS AGO, A writer-friend and I decided to start an e-mail correspondence on the theme of serendipity. It seemed like a way to get into some interesting terrain. In our many years of conversation, we always seemed to be taking up topics relating to coincidence—losing and finding, accident, and so on. We quickly found that our daily exchange began to put out branches in all directions—touching also on writing, photography, poets, the workings of influence, mentorship, and artistic inspiration. This back-and-forth took over a good part of the summer.

I bring this up now because looking back on this exchange in the wake of rereading *Speak, Memory*, I see thoughts owed to Nabokov, his way of thinking. For whatever reason, I didn't realize this at the time, even as I sometimes quoted him in my letters. Such are the subterranean workings of influence. The recognition of my debt came late.

I don't mean to suggest that I'd been borrowing Nabokov's ideas or expressions, but rather that my fascination with the subject, what drove me pursue my own intuition, turned out in many ways to echo the core Nabokovian worldview. And I realized how important it was to me. The summer-long exchange was something more than sport for me—it was a way to release impulses that had been a building pressure for years.

I admit to the deep affinity I feel with Nabokov's views on coincidence and pattern, and I feel grateful for the reinforcement they give me. He treats these things with full seriousness, as very much a part of the project of meaning. Is it possible for a non-believer to affirm that there *is* something more, that life is not just a scroll of days with one thing following another and erasing what has come before? These questions were all a part of our serendipity correspondence.

Though no believer himself, Nabokov was most determined in his private pursuit of meaning and closure. Throughout his work, and especially in the memoir, he conveys the active sense that life is a problem to be solved, a puzzle to be completed, a code to be deciphered. Reading him, I always get the deep-down feeling that there is somewhere to get to. A subtle teleology runs through his work. But though we do get hints about destination, they are never very explicit. No clear guidelines are offered. For my part, I want to know if it was enough for Nabokov to achieve a deep recovery of experience through the work of memory. Certainly this feels like the central ambition of *Speak, Memory*. Though what would mark a successful recovery? Is there some emotional closure to be found that finally banishes the void of loss and longing?

•

Obsessed as Nabokov is with memory, he is no less occupied with what he sees as the implications of pattern and design. He all but announces this right at the outset of the memoir:

> Neither in environment nor in heredity can I find the exact instrument that fashioned me, the anonymous roller that pressed upon my life a certain intricate watermark whose unique design becomes visible when the lamp of art is made to shine through life's foolscap.

And then, right after, adds: "The following of such thematic designs through one's life should be, I think, the true purpose of autobiography." If this is not an announcement of aesthetic redemption, I don't know what is.

These two sentences might actually be the most important in the book. For here Nabokov intimates that there *is* a unique design in an individual's life; he also suggests that art, in his case writing, can lead one toward its discovery. Asserting that the search for such designs can—ought to—comprise a life's work, Nabokov imparts to his memoir a sense of high personal mission. For while writing is, of course, an expression meant to be read by others, it is also a powerful instrument of exploration for the writer, maybe even leading him to discern the "unique design" of his life. *If* there is such a design. Nabokov believed there was.

How might writing light that lamp? Is there some kind of divining rod that gets extended as the writer traverses the unconscious? Such basic metaphors easily enlarge the range of suggestion, but I don't think that they offer any clues about how that process of illumination might work.

Contemplating creativity and the unconscious, we are in a zone of mysteries. No one has yet explained the nature of inspiration, or how it is that inner materials at a certain point insist on release. In ancient lore, the Muse was the intermediary figure, and if She were available for questioning, I would ask her what determines what she fetches up from the depths and organizes into art. Because the best inspired works are not just scattershot eruptions from the unconscious—they tend to come in shapes that often feel necessary, complete unto themselves. A sonneteer's inspirations often arrive in the form of sonnets, and so on. What brings together this and that, but not *that*? What is the shaping agency and how does it work? Nabokov's vigorous repudiation of Freud does not always make sense.

This idea of art turning materials from the chaotic unconscious into coherent expression may somehow be linked to this idea of finding closure. I don't know about "meaning," though I do use the word often. For while closure offers the abstract fulfillment—a circuit completed—meaning, to me, implies there is something more, something larger, to be said. It also presupposes that there is some entity or agency that confers that meaning. But what? If we don't allow any deity into the picture, what are we talking about?

Nabokov, I imagine, thought of meaning as intrinsic—as a complex felt connection between things that attests to inherent design, but that does not propose a designer. Just the indication of a coherent shape may be enough to dispel the fear of utter meaninglessness. And if the shape itself doesn't exist, the will of the individual to find one is a testimony unto itself. The question behind all other questions is: where does the desire for meaning come from?

Nabokov's pattern searches take several different forms. In *Speak, Memory,* we have the image of the folded carpet as well as the watermarked foolscap. The logic of both of these images suggests that the design is already there and can ideally be found using the lens of art. Or could it be that Nabokov was just giving in to the neatness of the analogy? I hate to think so, but it's a worthy question, because so many of his other pattern references are more about piecing together separate parts until they finally yield a design. A design which is either somehow intended, part of the deep premise of Nature, or else is created by some pattern-making gene we all carry.

This is a key distinction—a discovery of something pre-existing versus a fashioning of something from separate pieces. Coincidentally, we find a similar distinction set out in current theorizing about memory. The received wisdom has been the old school notion that the memory somewhere "exists," as if in a file, and that we have to work to recover it. Current neuroscience, by contrast, proposes that we don't find our memories so much as we create them from available neural traces. Which side would Nabokov come down on? Are both even possible?

Coincidence and serendipity certainly come into play in the Nabokovian universe, not so much in terms of the more outward sense of pattern-making, but more elusively as vital "events" in the process of discovering meaningful links, often enough between events that are far apart in space or time. Or both. One good example is the already-cited "theme of the matches."

Remember, the visiting Russian general, Kuropatkin, amuses the young Nabokov by lining up matches on the couch. Years later, in wartime circumstances, his father encounters his old friend, now disheveled and bundled up, in a crowded exodus, when he is approached for a light. The "theme of the matches."

Episodes like this tantalize because they bring us to what feels like a brink of meaning, but never quite carry us over. They do, however, convey the feeling of the "uncanny." The fact of that wintry encounter is clearly significant—but in what way? Another narrator might offer it as a curious aside, whereas Nabokov remarks it with pointed interest and names it. That naming shows that the event has been taken up by the writer's patterning intelligence; it becomes suggestive—but of what? Of strange twists of destiny, of meanings that exceed our basic logical grasp? What else could it be? The effect it creates is that there is *something* behind the ongoing flow of circumstance. That feeling—inkling—brings some reassurance, though it's not exactly clear why.

The other, possibly more plausible, way to think of this, is that though the events are ultimately nothing more than happenstance, we ourselves have such a powerful need to make them form some pattern—*mean* something. In Nabokov's case that need would have been extraordinarily powerful. But behind every answer or explanation another *why?* rears up. How do we account for that specific drive, how did it find its way into our DNA, and what are the implications of feeling such a need? So far as we know, no other life-form has a bent toward understanding itself.

The most telling and resonant of Nabokov's various patternings comes at the very end of the memoir. While the conceit is fascinating in itself, its placement clinches it as Nabokov's last word on the matter. And while the anecdote is not exactly "conclusive evidence" of anything, it does leave the reader finishing the memoir in a state of metaphysical conjecturing.

This scene, pages from the end, has Nabokov stepping forth as a married man and a father, though all of this family business has happened off-stage. The three Nabokovs—our author, his wife Vera, and their young son Dmitri—are staying at the seaside at Biarritz, waiting to get the papers needed to emigrate to America. The spark for Nabokov's fantasy comes as young Dmitri runs to show his father a glazed shard of majolica he has found on the shore. Studying it, Nabokov suddenly fancies that it might exactly fit to a piece that he himself had found when he was three on the same beach. He then goes on in his imagination to fit those two to a third that his mother had found on that beach in 1882, and then again with a piece found by *her* mother long decades before, "and so on, until this assortment of parts, if all had been preserved, might have been put together to make the complete, the absolutely complete, bowl, broken by some Italian child, God knows where and when, and now mended by these rivets of bronze."

Of course, this is a pure piece of fancy, conveying both mystery and exactitude—very Borgesian in this way. Nabokov is voicing overtly his desire for the restoration of something that has been broken. And though his conceit is a pure imagining, it tells so much about the man. Not only in terms of his thinking about his life, but also bringing a number of his preoccupations and themes together into a single emblematic parable. Time, which is at the heart of everything he writes, is of course at the heart of the scene. The great lapsed increments are part of his conceit, in which reassembling something long shattered is a metaphor for the work of joining the lost parts of his family past into a unity. The imagined fulfillment comes right at the point when he and his own family are poised to start a new life.

Where most of Nabokov's brooding about life, destiny, and uniquely inscribed patterns has been centered on his own private experience, this closing passage about the majolica shards takes a different perspective. The joining of the pieces edge to edge moves back in time to encompass his whole extended lineage, and thus allows him to view his own life as a piece to be fitted to all the others. The widening perspective, coming where it does, where he is seen with his wife and son, also subtly harkens us back to the time before his own arrival into his family—the arrival which was, in effect, the filling of the gap represented by the empty pram by the door.

The shards in this late passage are fastened into place by rivets of bronze, which are metaphorically the connections forged by imagination and artistic inspiration. However, the bowl itself—mended—does not signify beyond itself. It is a broken thing restored—and no longer in its original pristine shape. Yet in Nabokov's hands it becomes a new-made thing that somehow represents the redemption of the whole family. It's a bold imaginative stroke. While I understand it as a fanciful imagining, I respond to it as something more significant—as a gratifying metaphor for a very real psychological process. The artistic rightness of the image somehow overrides its literal implausibility.

How do the opening and closing images of *Speak, Memory* relate? Nabokov begins, as we know, with the now-famous spatial picture of existence, which he features, also with an image, as a crack of light between two infinite darknesses. From this detached and distanced perspective, a life is almost a nothing, a mere flash. But of course, the memoir that follows belies this notion entirely. The opening pages show us the boy living in luxury, cosseted by family and governesses—everything is close-up, completely intimate, portrayed via impressions and sensations. So many prized details are rendered in high-resolution close-up; so many moments distend into duration. And events throughout the memoir are seen to connect across time in a way that strongly suggests that life is more than just a succession of transitory events. Which is to say, no mere crack of light.

Time can only be redeemed symbolically through art, and, in Nabokov's special case, through an art that makes that redemption its main preoccupation. The fitting together of the majolica pieces at the end makes the memoir feel like a puzzle that has finally been completed. In that sense, it's like a game—a serious game, but a game nonetheless. We should remember, though, that the nature of any game is to create a closed circle of high attention, so that whoever participates—here it is the reader—is drawn away from all daily concerns. But we should also acknowledge that the memoir is not any real redemption for the reader. Rather, it is an oasis of duration, which does end. Closing the covers, that reader looks up to find herself back in the world.

It's harder to say what the business of concluding means to the writer, who obviously also knows that creative immersion is not perpetual, but who also finds in concluding a sense of a circuit closed. The threads are gathered together. This seems to me far stronger and deeper than whatever the reader gets to feel. At the end of Woolf's *To the Lighthouse*, the painter Lily Briscoe, who has been working on one painting for years—from the very beginning of her annual stay with the Ramsays—finally has the flash, an abstract insight about color and placement that finally allows her to finish. Those formal considerations of shape and color obviously stand in for a good deal more. Lily exclaims: "I have had my vision!" And that "vision," abstract in its outline, but emotional in its content, is what allows her to put closure to her long obsession with Mrs. Ramsey, the central figure in the novel.

With that one moment, Woolf's artistic skill persuades us that art *is* redemption. Not of a life, but of unresolved emotion. Lily has broken free from an inward domination; she can move on. What is so interesting—and also confirming—is what Woolf wrote in her diaries. She confessed that when she had finished writing *To the Lighthouse*, she felt she had finally laid her own mother to rest. She, too, had achieved closure by proxy.

Art has that power. The question I would have posed to Nabokov is whether through writing the memoir he had in some meaningful way "finished" with his childhood and young manhood. Had he dealt with the losses of exile and thus freed himself for a second life? His closing image suggests so. We are shown the author spotting a "splendid ship's funnel" rising behind the rooftops of Biarritz. It is, of course, the ship that will take him to America. His voice here is fresh, full of anticipation.

How does this "completion" work? Was it for Nabokov the reclaiming of the long-ago lost days, or was it a way to lay them to rest by giving them a finished form? I think of the often-repeated wisdom that writing one's memories drains them of their emotional power. But how does this happen? My theory is that neither the reclaiming of memories nor the laying to rest happens just because the writer's inner content has been shaped and exteriorized. What matters just as much—and I have this from experience—is the hard psychological work that creates the transformation from life to art.

That deep work, then, is not just the writing itself, but also the rallying and sustaining of the energy and concentration required to re-enter the past at a deep enough level. The writing on the page may be descriptive and certainly requires labor to make it "work," but to get to the place where those descriptions feel authentic and not just decoratively applied requires recovery of the actual emotion. In this way, it is related to the work of therapy. Here I think of Robert Frost's phrase: "No tears in the writer, no tears in the reader." I'm talking not just about the emotion that was originally part of the recollected experience, but also the emotion that comes from the long exertion of going back to the past. Insofar as that past is lost, regaining it in memory is profound. But how this exertion changes—or actually lays to rest—the original sorrow of the loss may never be clear.

I'm guessing that Nabokov felt ambivalence about artistically shaping his memories. A written scene is, in a sense, the death mask of the experience. And while there is naturally a powerful impulse to come to terms with the past, there might also be a contrary desire, or need, to keep the wound fresh. This is not a simple psychological transaction. Coming to terms with the past—alongside the catharsis of the expression itself—is also necessarily a modification. The recovered past is inevitably modified at every point, if only for more effective aesthetic presentation. Eventually, though, that new or slightly altered version supplants the original memory, or else changes it significantly. This is not unlike what happens after we see a movie adapted from a novel— we may later find that we've lost purchase on the original.

Nabokov would probably not have been willing to preserve all his memories etherized and pinned like butterflies. He would have wanted to preserve some of the tension of the unresolved. For it is that tension—that feeling of things yet unresolved—that drives the writer to write. One cannot work with inert materials.

This might be yet one more explanation of Nabokov's great reticence about family. Maybe he wanted to preserve the emotional core of those bonds. What a paradox to ponder: that a writer would write a memoir in order to preserve parts of the past, but then would also leave certain things out—in order to preserve them.

The Shape of a Life

TIME-OBSESSED, NABOKOV USES THE elasticity of his medium to explore how time has worked in his life. Memoirists, as we know, proceed in various ways. Some keep to a basic chronology, while others jump back and forth from the writer's present to select moments of the past. Structure expresses how the mind works. Nabokov uses various approaches. One is his very effective way of flashing forward abruptly from one point in time in order to give a glimpse of a person's destiny. For example, he views his long-time tutor, a man named Lenski, in forward-flashing destiny-time. "In 1919," he writes, "the Bolsheviks came and turned off the lights, and Lensky fled to France . . ." Then he tells us, "he was said to be earning a precarious living on the Riviera by painting pictures on seashells and stones."

Nabokov's way of infiltrating the ongoing narrative with these strategic time-shifts gives us new perspectives. It also forces us to take different view of the figures who are glimpsed in what will be their future. But the main effect for me is finally subliminal. The structural openness to various time-frames conveys the sense that we are experiencing time as a kind of totality—from something like a God's-eye view. Correlative with that is the fact that lives seen inhabiting several narrative tenses are more easily understood as destinies—which, I'm quite sure, Nabokov intended.

As Nabokov can in some instances hyper-magnify small episodes into important scenes and then in others account for whole years with a few sentences, so he also calls on the future when he feels the need. For the reader, there is no discernible pattern, no method. Writing out of his present, years after the events he is narrating, Nabokov at times freely mixes sequences and chronologies according to his needs—which themselves are not always known to others.

Done well, these maneuvers can have powerful effects, especially where a person's final end is revealed. If we are reading about someone, and then learn—from what almost feels like an aside—that the person will one day years hence be killed in a battle, our whole feeling about what we are reading necessarily changes. It's the García Márquez effect found at the very beginning of *One Hundred Years of Solitude,* when he writes: "Many years later, as he faced the firing squad, Colonel Aureliano Buendia was to remember that distant afternoon when his father took him to discover ice . . ." Our conventional sense of time advancing—past to present to future—is abruptly penetrated.

With Nabokov's forward leaps, meanwhile, we are reminded that what we're reading is all a hindsight view, that it represents the narration of his somewhat capricious memory rather than any more neutral sort of recounting. As far as the narrative itself, the character is moved from simple time, which is always confined to its moment, to destiny-time, which apprehends the life in that God's-eye view that presumes to be all-seeing.

Vantage is crucial. It is the first thing the would-be memoirist has to decide on because there is no proceeding without it. The discovery—for that's what it can feel like—is not always easy. I taught personal essay and memoir in various venues over the years, and when my students were not sure how to begin, I would often suggest that they first center on a moment from their present lives, and then from that seek out a detail that would be an associative trigger to the past. As often as not, that trigger would point the way—it would reveal what they didn't know they wanted to say. To others I might recommend that they imagine the essay in terms of alternating sections—one of these moving a current-day narrative along, the other using the past as a counterpoint.

I say this only to underscore the absolute importance of having a time structure, a way of situating events. This conception is what gives shape to the narrative and sets the subjective pace. Nabokov, so fascinated by patterns, is tricky in this way. His own structure(s) can feel deceptively improvisatory, offering no clear blueprint for how the work will proceed. How are we to map his progress? He begins *Speak, Memory* on a quasi-philosophical note—proposing that our lives are but an interval of light, between infinities of darkness. From there, he introduces himself, as a soon-to-be arrival, which he conveys by his focus on the image of an as-yet-empty pram waiting by the door. Then, with a few quick strides, he moves us from that eerie phase of anticipation and presents himself as a *fait accompli*: a very young child. Soon enough, he is in his boyhood years, creating richly detailed scenes centered on his various governesses and tutors—and, yes, now and then flashing forward to tell us what finally became of them. There is no anchoring "plot." As to the vantage of his American life, he never really establishes either the locale or year of the writing; he gives us almost no indicators. The effect of this is that we, his readers, have no clear point of orientation, but it also means that we are that much freer to follow such leaps in time as Nabokov does make.

I do wonder how impulsive his time shifts finally are, whether they really follow some undisclosed plan or are just obeying the writer's impetuous inspiration. Of course, I want to believe that they are carefully thought out—for they exert such powerful subliminal effects on me as I read. The power of tenses, certainly in the hands of a writer as time-obsessed as Nabokov, is considerable. Tenses control not just what we know about when, but they enable a view of the life that is somehow more four-dimensional than what we find in most works in the genre.

With a single time-leap—"Many years later . . ."—the whole reading assumption changes. With that single stroke

we are in the hands of a lowercase god, one to whom everything is known. There is a certain exhilaration in taking
that leap, but then we do also face the narrative differently.
Walter Benjamin, in an essay on the idea of the storyteller,
quotes Moritz Heimann, who wrote "A man who dies at the
age of thirty-five is at every point of his life a man who dies
at the age of thirty-five." It is, again, the godlike perspective. As a reader, I find this awareness changes everything.
As soon as I learn what will happen to a character in the
future, I can't help but interpret everything relating to that
character in that light.

The Persistence of Memory

MEMORY IS THE INDISPUTABLE FOUNDATION and impetus of memoir—the roots of the words are inextricably entwined. So every memoir ought to begin with the words: *I remember.* How the book is written, what form it takes—everything can be traced back to the character of the person remembering and the nature of the memories recalled. Nor should we forget that in this genre every memory is a creative act: it has been edited, compressed (or expanded), staged, and as there are few other corroborating sources to appeal to, the version is usually accepted as definitive by default.

No memoir can offer anything like a neutral account of past experience—there is no such thing. The author is always up to something—whether setting the record straight on some matter(s), ennobling or avenging him- or herself, illuminating some important event, personal or public . . . Deep and partly-unconscious impulses drive the narrative. When I wrote my memoir, I was, on the face of it, trying to understand my formation in terms of family past and childhood influences. I saw that as my main mission. But now, years later, I see so clearly that other impulses were driving me as well—I was settling certain accounts, trying to cast my experiences in an "interesting" light, etc.

Nabokov was, I believe, bent on two things. For one, he obviously needed to tell his story in the light of the core trauma of his life. He did this not by focusing on the drama of that separation, but rather by working his way back through memories and trying to restore sensations and important moments. But I also believe that he was, on a more formal level, conducting a literary experiment in which proportion, space, and degree of detail were all to be determined by purely subjective criteria. Nabokov knew that the inner life keeps its own time. It also observes its own sense of scale.

Persona and Person

THE PUBLIC IMAGE OF NABOKOV is of a brilliant and eccentric Russian émigré, who became the very emblem of cosmopolitan sophistication, with his half-whimsical hauteur and curmudgeonly manner. He had that plummy pronunciation with its rolling r's and vaguely British accent. There is, of course, that vein of drollness that runs through most of his work—we can feel the slightly raised eyebrow in certain more ornate expressions. The man also had a genuine fastidiousness about accuracy, which we see in his absolute insistence on the rightness of his idioms in his translation of Pushkin's *Eugene Onegin*. He took this so far that his intransigence about certain key matters of expression led him to part ways with his former friend and admirer—Edmund Wilson.

The reader just coming to *Speak, Memory* might be aware of some of these things, but for the readers who are not, most of these character formations can be deduced from reading.

I count off these attributes because Nabokov was a

famous man with a distinctive image in the public mind. They are, not surprisingly, aspects of his essential character—a character he sometimes played to, both in public appearances and, more slyly, in his memoir. I do get the sense, especially when he is depicting his younger years, that he is often writing out of a persona. The *tell*, or giveaway, is the archness, a playfulness of tone that suggests he is admiring his own performance, considering himself from a bemused distance. The word *performance* is key here, for it suggests the self-division that characterizes the person who puts on some kind of show for the public. Looking back on his "inspired" poem, he writes, "It seems hardly worthwhile to add that, as themes go, my elegy dealt with the loss of a beloved mistress—Delia, Tamara, or Lenore—whom I had never lost, never loved, never met, but was all set to meet, love, lose." How fondly he sets the record straight.

Stage performance is, of course, exaggeration, and there is naturally a gap between truth and presentation. To some degree, this self-division is true of the memoirist as well.

I don't think that any memoir finally achieves what we consider authenticity. Though people do tend to think of a memoir as a kind of unveiling—as the *real* story—this is almost never the case. Every writer poses; and every memoir is in significant ways a fiction. Writers who don't have an identifiable public persona might exaggerate or else censor things simply to make a better story. I can't believe that Nabokov, who had such a distinct—and by this point established—public persona, could have avoided playing off that image, whether by reinforcing it, or trying to counter it in devious ways. An image is, after all, a kind of captivity.

It might seem that I'm chiding the man for not telling it straight, but I'm not. There is, as I keep insisting, no straight telling—and if there were, who would pronounce on that straightness? A scrupulously accurate fact-based portrayal might provide a map of the events of the life, but it would say nothing about the person who lived it. As Virginia Woolf wrote, "So they say, 'This is what happened,' but they do not say what the person was like to whom it happened." The person is everything.

Reading *Speak, Memory*, with all its elisions, foreshortenings, and magnifications, we only get aspects of the life— that's a given—but no one can say that we don't get Nabokov. The memoir offers a literarily amplified version of the man, of course, but one can read *through* the amplifications and winnow out the camouflaged self—the self that would go about eliding, foreshortening, and magnifying in just these ways.

Coda: Concluding
Unscientific Postscript

I HAVE TRIED TO ACCOUNT for many of the things that
have drawn me to *Speak, Memory*, and now I ask myself if
I've gotten to the most basic point of connection. That I
should even ask suggests that maybe I haven't, that there
is still something central I want to say. In fact, there is.
It's both simple and diffuse. For while I have tried to deal
squarely with the parts—the different aspects of Nabokov's
memoir—I have not dealt with the underlying sensibility
that those parts arise from, and how my sense of *that* has
influenced me more than anything else. What I am gestur-
ing toward is not a *thing*. It's more like the writer's deeper
disposition, his character, his worldview.

•

If there has been one main subject in my own writing, aside
from literary essays and memoir, it has been the sweeping
cultural transition we have gone through in my lifetime

and are going through now with continuing momentum. I mean, of course, our nearly full-scale migration from analog to digital, and everything that has followed from it—all the behaviors, attitudes, and cultural assumptions—and their deeper human implications.

My literary involvement with this topic began decades ago. I remember the specific first occasion. It was the early seventies. I was still in college at the time, but as Ann Arbor was only forty miles away, I often came home on weekends to visit my family. The visit I'm thinking of now was in the late fall—I know this because the trees were bare of leaves and the air was sharp and clear. I had gone out after dinner for a walk in the old neighborhood, and at some point found myself on top of the highest hill in the area. I meant to get a good look at the night sky, but I actually ended up doing another kind of beholding. For when I finally lowered my gaze from the constellations, I faced something almost as remarkable. Slowly panning the neighborhood, I saw blue lights pulsing everywhere, the flashes coming in strange syncopation. These were all TVs, of course, but our neighbors were obviously watching different channels. But they were *watching*—every house. I remember I stood there for a long time. I had the feeling that I was right on the brink of something.

This was my first wake-up moment—my unexpected vision of how television was insinuating itself into our lives. Of course, Marshall McLuhan had offered his assessment years before—his slogan was "the medium is the message"—but for me it was new. And though my thoughts about those ubiquitous screens were at that time only about television, they would eventually lead me to contemplate other screens—and a whole cultural transformation that was taking place. The first essay I wrote about this was titled, referentially, "Television: The Medium in the Mass Age."

Before long, the personal computer—clunky as yet—arrived and quickly furthered what TV had started. The proliferation of sophisticated and addictive interfaces was something new in the world. I could feel the digital momentum building even as most people were acting as if it were all business as usual. When I ventured my thoughts and doubts, the response I often got was, in effect, "Lighten up! This is progress." I was not so sure. To me these screens represented the arrival of a whole new electronic culture; they created a different landscape. And people appeared spellbound—I saw on many faces a particular abstracted expression I had not seen much before, a focus into some middle distance. Naturally, I thought about hypnosis, passivity, brainwashing—all of those supposedly dystopian effects Orwell and Huxley had written about. Was *this* what they were getting at? I'm sure I dramatized the situation, but looking back I can also see that there were truths to be extracted.

I was still writing essays and literary criticism back then—it was the late eighties—but in those pieces I was already making frequent references to what I felt was the pressure of these changes. I paid close attention to the writers who seemed to be tuning in to what was happening. I

read Marshall McLuhan, George W. S. Trow, Don DeLillo, Richard Powers, Walker Percy, and David Foster Wallace— all men, alas—but they were taking on the issues that concerned all of us: media, artificial intelligence, social alienation and threats to selfhood.

After enough of these sidebar reflections in literary essays, I felt the push to write more directly, and for a year or two I did just that. It was the right time for these thoughts. The essays I was writing eventually shaped themselves into a book, which was published as *The Gutenberg Elegies: The Fate of Reading in an Electronic Age*. It was, as the title suggests, a lament. But while it did center on threats to reading, it was also asking how the new dispensation was influencing the ways we think and act—and live. My use of the word *elegies* in the title was deliberate. I was worried—as I still am— that we were losing many age-old habits and customs and replacing them far too quickly—and it was not quite clear with what.

My essays, now chapters, reflected on the erosion of our attention spans, the loss of "deep time," and the destruction of all contexts by the new information glut. My thoughts were, no surprise, often derided, especially in certain "progressive" quarters. This was not what people wanted to hear just then— digital progress was the new excitement and who wanted the opinions of the carping critic? But for all that, some useful debate was sparked. Soon enough, I was branded as a Luddite, which I took as an honorific, even though I knew it was cultural code for someone who opposed progress and initiative.

But times change and things have evolved. The older I got and the further our technologies advanced, the more I understood that this is not a yes/no question, but a situation with a great many shades and qualifications. My original view was basically binary. I ended *The Gutenberg Elegies* with the words: "Refuse it!" and I used that for a while as my somewhat hyperbolic credo—though it was exactly the response I then advocated. These days, I don't think that anyone, myself included, still imagines that a reversal of course is even possible. When I was asked to write a preface for a new edition of the book some years later, I opened by confessing that I'd had to make adjustments. Mostly I blamed my children—but of course that was a thin excuse. I had conceded to the non-negotiables for getting on in the world.

I write out of hindsight now. Back in the eighties, before the laptop and high-powered search engines, everything was new and unpredictable. I wondered if we might still somehow reverse course. No. The operative principle was something called Moore's Law, which showed convincingly that the processing power of the microchip was doubling every year. With each doubling, the larger system, including the Internet, was more deeply digitized. And then—was there a moment?—everything tipped.

My focus kept changing as more and more of our societal operations made use of high-speed processing. ATM machines eliminated the need to stand in line waiting for the bank teller. The racheting fax machine was displaced by computer transmission, and the old reliable landline quickly gave way to ever-more-portable cell phones. Who would object to these time-saving and streamlining technologies? I did, for a time—until, as was inevitable, there was no resisting. Everyone needed a computer and a cell phone, no getting around it. It was the so-called "slippery slope"—we were all on it to some degree. I should have guessed that there was more to come.

I apologize for this extended recap, but the larger progression matters here, and does eventually relate to Nabokov.

The ongoing leaps of digital innovation created all kinds of ripple effects, some of them momentous. The arrival of the fully loaded iPhone was a case in point. Here was a pocket-sized implement with screen, typing keys, internet access, as well as camera and sound—it was the very pinnacle of digital possibility. These smart and empowering portable devices quickly penetrated the culture, and though quite pricey were taken up even by the disadvantaged populations. The truth, clear to everyone, it seems, was that one could not really be a part of society if not *in* the network.

This iPhone technology got increasingly sophisticated. Even the so-called "digerati" had trouble keeping current. Applications, now called "apps," were popping up by the hour, each one representing an expansion of connective possibilities. People could now track each other, do their banking, order food, get news, summon rides, play games, watch movies, send photos and texts, count their steps, and on and on. It was all so easy—instant and virtual. Users could spend much of the time formerly given over to "real world" activities at an ethereal remove. The ability to engage with other users while sitting alone at home was just one of so many new life-options. The formerly defining frictional interface between man and world began to erode.

The nuances of these innovations would further explain why Nabokov is so important to me, but I think even this basic outline is enough. It describes the terms of the battle between singularity and standardization, between electronic collectivism and what is uniquely individual.

I started to theorize the emergence of this ulterior reality a while back. As with those blue lights, I can more or less pinpoint my moment of awakening. I was in my car on my way home from Boston University, where I work. This was several years ago now. I had stopped at a red light on Commonwealth Avenue, right near the campus center. It was noon, class break, and I waited, staring distractedly at the crowd swarming all around my car. And then, who knows why, I felt that distraction collapse. I saw what was in front of me, and in a matter of a minute I started getting a suddenly vivid update on the state of things—what we had come to and where we clearly were headed.

What I saw in those few minutes—green lights don't matter at midday on campus—were literally hundreds of people of the same age streaming in front of me as if in lock-step, every last one of them bent forward in the archetypal posture of the iPhone user—and emerging Homo Sapiens— telegraphing with body language and distracted expressions that their attention was utterly elsewhere. It was not that I had never seen iPhone users walking—I saw them every day—but the herd aspect was a great magnifier. This scene was a collective "not-being-here" that was a thing unto itself. At that moment, I couldn't help but picture Steve Jobs's famous 1984 Super Bowl ad. Though Jobs's pitch showed a hammer hurled to break the screen visage of Big Brother addressing a crowd of mesmerized clones, what I had retained was the image of the clones.

Compressed moments like this can be decisive for the mind's grasping of a situation. Where the scatter of blue window-lights had woken me to see the huge inroads television had made in our culture, this moment at the intersection showed me that my fears of societal group-think were not without foundation.

Waiting there behind the wheel, I saw the hive behavior—the body postures, the lockstep movement—and I felt the almost magnetic indispensability of those little screens, the power of their compulsion. What I also took away—even more disconcerting—was the sense that there was now a kind of plasma between screen users and the material order we all still move through—"plasma TV" now seems more like a premonition than a product description.

I had thought and written about the hive mentality before but I had never seen its actual manifestation close up like this. I am, by nature, full of foreboding. I conjugate the trends I see, and what I always seem to arrive at is the scenario of a standardized society in which individuality is an ever-scarcer attribute, and inwardness—the great individualizer—is broadly depreciated. This is my version of a brave new world, and I take it seriously. I'm watching it happen. The more deeply we engage the circuitry—the vaporous "cloud"—the more we sacrifice, like the immediacy of experience, the capacity for sustained attention, and the will to independent action. The circuitry creates the hive. When we log on, we join a system.

Smart design and algorithms have figured most everything out. The only way we can get to the many things we need to get to is by mapping our vital facts into a prescribed grid. Online, we have to complete the field exactly to specifications, and even a single misplaced initial will keep us out. This is not to mention the dozens of essential codes we all need to keep track of. When we do fill in the blanks correctly, we are accepted into the fold, and inevitably we feel we are competent citizens. But to win this acceptance we have had to trade off our information and any number of points of personal access. Entering our statistics in the appointed fields, we become, at least for that company, a statistic ourselves. I won't even start in here about corporate mining of our information, never mind actual forms of surveillance.

I occasionally get a bit extreme on these matters, but as the old adage goes: even paranoids have enemies. It's hard for me not to picture a future where we can only deal with taxes, insurance, and medical providers—our essential societal needs—when our personal data and code references are all "accurate." That future is pretty much the present. Anyone who has ever sat fuming in front of a screen that

won't give access—that keeps flashing *invalid*—has to wonder what it would feel like to be invalidated, canceled, across
the board. "We're sorry but—."

These innovations are naturally promoted as benign.
They speed up so many formerly cumbersome actions, but
they also allow our privacy to be hacked and create a kind of
surveillance consciousness that impinges on our choices and
actions. Ceaseless advertiser messaging and the uniformity
of these grids enroll us in the collective slipstream. As links
and near-instantaneous transmissions combine to simulate a
perpetual present, we are at great risk of becoming creatures
of surface rather than depth. Interaction with the relentless
digital systems can only erode the inner life—the base on
which our individuality finally rests.

I was just writing out these thoughts on our situation
when—serendipitously—I came upon this quotation from
Jaron Lanier. Lanier is one of the proclaimed digital gurus,
but a guru whose critiques are often as serious as his advoca-
cies. In the passage I found, he is reflecting on this very issue:

> We're headed toward a world where people are
> being partially programmed by algorithms. A lot of
> what you'll do during the day will be designed and
> set up and contextualized and motivated by algo-
> rithms. You see, algorithms don't really work. So in
> order for a predictive algorithm to work, the only
> way to get that effect is for the people to change in
> order to make the algorithm smarter. Everybody

will have to conform to whatever behavior is needed to make the algorithms appear to gave been correct.

Lanier's analysis is chilling in the extreme: our now-indispensible systems are being created so that we *have* to bend to them. We have no other choice. And the long-term effect of our bending is to unify, or, more accurately, "standardize" our actions—and, to some extent, our lives. The specter of mass conformity that was such a topic in the fifties and sixties threatens to return, only this time bolstered by the incomprehensible power of networks—I think of them as "obedience networks"—that are like nothing we've ever seen.

Why am I saying all this? My anxious scenario of systems and conformity reveals much about who I am as a person, and all this background might help to explain my affinities and—going to the main point—why I knew so quickly that *Speak, Memory* was the book I wanted to write about. It is, I realize, a long way from Nabokov's world of memories to these premonitions of group-think, but my way of connecting them is obvious and direct. I'm talking about an outlook that calls on all of my experience and thinking and that shapes my subjective life. My outlook is who I am. Naturally, it informs all my reading—not just what I read, but how I read as well. And reading, for me, is a way of interacting with the world as a private self.

In view of this assessment of digital conformity, I can

say that Nabokov's sensibility, his way of seeing and expressing his world, has had an undeniable influence on my own
way of seeing and expressing—as well as my impulse to resist.

What *is* sensibility? It's a word not much heard these
days. When we do hear, it's most often as a kind of catch-all
word for a person's basic tastes and leanings, what might be
called his emotional consciousness.

Not everyone needs or even wants to develop a sensibility in this more "artistic" way, but artists and their serious audiences do share this attribute, and some meeting
of those separate sensibilities—a kind of Venn overlap—is
right at the heart of most aesthetic experience. Not everyone likes everything, of course, be it a book, painting, or
musical composition. The conventional wisdom is *de gust-
ibus disputandum non est*: there's no disputing taste, which
can be seen as the outward expression of sensibility. Where
the writer's and reader's tastes coincide there is an exchange
of vital energies. With books we are really drawn to there is
a sense of relationship. We are compelled by a verbal presence that greets us from the page and the contact feels not
just literary, but human.

Attracted as I am by so many of its aspects, the real
draw of *Speak, Memory* for me is the language and what
its active variations represent. I am back to sensibility, the
sounds, syntax, voice, pacing and other features that make
up Nabokov's prose style. As the old aphorism has it, "The
style is the man." Or woman. The person. With Nabokov,
the style, its insistent and personal precision, reveals an

unapologetic uniqueness that I find in very few authors. I'm not talking so much about the contents of the expression as about what the expression itself signals. In a word: individuality. Individuality that is an insistence on the specificity of the self, its impulses and prerogatives. It is manifest in the prose and, obviously, in the man himself.

The simplicity of the style-is-the-man assertion belies an underlying complexity. Because all of those particulars—syntax, etc.—that make every writer's expression his or her own, do not appear out of nowhere. They naturally reflect some aspect of that writer's essential makeup. Pacing on the page, for instance, is certainly linked to biology as well as psychology, whereas syntax maps to the mind's way of structuring reality. Hemingway was famously terse in his constructions, while Henry James could not refrain from qualifying most any expression. Neither by temperament would be capable of writing like the other.

What Nabokov's prose tells us is that he is a writer hyper-alert to minutiae, complex in his way of perceiving connections between things, able to hold emotion at a distance and to refract it, and also that he seeks out likeness and makes surprising metaphoric transformations. Other attributes need to be considered as well: the bent toward romanticizing and striking the lyric note, a fastidiousness about details and a self-regarding confidence that can feel like snobbism, right alongside a most vulnerable nostalgia. Any writer's prose can be characterized thus according to its presenting tendencies. The exercise might well expose commonalities with others, but also, significantly, differences, and the sum total of all findings would give us a kind of psychological fingerprint, unlike anyone else's.

I read Nabokov to indulge myself in shared affinities and to savor his special way with words and images, but the deeper reason—linked, of course—is the basic corroboration offered by his worldview. I feel unusually in tune with the inner man that his style represents. I go to Nabokov is to remind myself of the power and necessity of inwardness. I turn to him when I want to reaffirm that neither the world presented to me nor the societally-presumed outlook on life is a given. To me, Nabokov has always represented the self, that never-to-be-duplicated fingerprint of identity. He stands for Individuality fought for and earned.

My own private search is ultimately philosophical—how should I choose to live and what should be my terms of meaning? I look everywhere for confirmation. As is obvious, I have my recurrent night thoughts. I worry about how we might secure a meaningful sense of self in the light of the ways that the world is changing. What will happen to subjective identity and what will be the relation of private to public? Can the inner life survive the standardizing onslaught?

My bent is dystopian, I know. But I also know there is no way to find the evidence that will validate my imaginings. We can only ponder the lives we are living and compare our times to former times. It's obvious to me that we are placing the former "real"—material—world at a distance. This is something new. We are experiencing less reality-traction than before. Our perpetual distraction undermines our sense of inwardness and also downplays the idea of its mattering. Where do we then find the psychological resources we need to resist the pressures of power? Not in science—of that I'm sure.

My views, formed in the pre-digital era, were based on certain assumptions—givens. I studied the humanities for years, and I embraced Emerson's imperative to create a true and unique self, as well as the idea that wisdom and meaning can be struggled for and achieved. The arts were clearly vital to this. Reading Orwell and Huxley in college, I shuddered at their visions—of a robotic citizenry, of complete social control by systems, of helpless capitulation to enforced norms. When I was in school I saw these as exaggeratedly paranoid fantasies, not as actual threats. Now I understand how deeply they have infiltrated my thinking.

I consider *Speak, Memory* to be a private existential guide leading the way in this massive reconfiguration of values —an antidote to many of my fears. Just opening the book starts to refresh my convictions. Nabokov's prose gives me a world of inward possibility—a belief that there are meanings to be discovered and patterns to be remarked. It underscores and enacts the importance of attention, which is not just a mode of approaching things, but is also how we recognize the variety and intricacy of all things. Attention shows us the finely drawn markings on the wings of a moth. The memoir is a place hospitable to private contemplation and all that is unique unto itself.

Speak, Memory

I CLOSE WITH A SLIGHTLY embarrassing admission. I read every page of Nabokov's memoir any number of times, and even studied the estate maps that decorate the front and back inside cover. I took in everything, it seems, but the title. Though I've cited it who knows how often in these pages, it strikes me that I never *read* it. By which I mean that I never slowed down enough to consider what it was saying.

Only the other day, as I was bringing my project to a close, did I get it. Nabokov takes care with his titles, as he takes care with everything that he puts to page. He obviously thought about this one enough to change the name of the book from the original, *Conclusive Evidence*. I'm not sure why he chose to do this. But this new title, now as I contemplate it, seems far more apt. Simply, obviously, Nabokov is giving a command: he is ordering memory to say what *it* has to say. Which is significant if you think about it—as if it's not Nabokov the social person and citizen deciding on what account to give, but rather the inner soul. That soul is, for these purposes, Mnemosyne. The Muse of memory itself is telling what *she* knows.

Coda:
Fact-Checking the Memoirist

WHEN I SET OUT TO write about *Speak, Memory*, I resolved to focus strictly on the book and to try to discover what experiences and thoughts of mine might have created such strong personal bond. I kept away from biographies, studies, critical opinions, and so on, though I did, as I acknowledge, come to my task with an amateur's sense of who this writer was.

I wanted my response to be as unadulterated as possible. Wanting to read (reread) the memoir as it was intended to be read, I sealed myself off from the opinions and theories of others.

It was only when I finished putting down my thoughts that I turned to the first volume of Brian Boyd's comprehensive two-part biography, *Vladimir Nabokov: The Russian Years*. At this point, I was fascinated to see how certain episodes and relationships were treated by a scholar intent on being objective, and who had access to papers and diaries and so on. What I found was, for me, eye-opening. Nabokov, it appears, took a number of liberties with some of the events he described. If Mnemosyne spoke, it was with a writer's instinct for making effective scenes. This did not fully surprise me—the man was, after all, an artificer of the first rank—but it set out the difference between lyric memoir—my focus here—and the scrupulous accounting of what is actually known. Boyd's account made clear to me the gulf between the so-called "letter of the law" and the "spirit of the law." What might this mean about all I had written?

I decided to zero in on several important scenes, comparing Nabokov's portrayal with what Boyd reported. Almost right away I felt myself tossed around. What I had been presenting as the baffling nature of the writer's treatment of family, for instance, baffled me no longer. So far his responses to the deaths of his parents went, I was relieved to read the "truth." Privately, away from the page—not surprisingly—Nabokov had suffered both deeply and had expressed himself emotionally.

Boyd quotes a long passage from a diary entry by Nabokov from the time just after his father's death. He sets out the sequence of events, how it was that the news arrived, and then flashes back to the last hours he spent with him. "The night before he had been so happy," he writes. "He laughed, he fought with me when I began to demonstrate a boxing clinch." As everyone was readying for bed, his father had helped him put his trousers in a press, and then, as they said goodnight, Nabokov asked him for the day's newspapers, which his father then passed through the gap between the parted doors. Writes Nabokov, "I didn't even see his hands. And I remember, that movement seemed creepy, ghostly—as if the sheets had thrust themselves through . . . —and the next morning Father set off for *Rul'* before I woke and I didn't see him again."

Reading this confirmed my supposition that it was not so much familial distance determining the presentation as the need to shield the privacy of those who were dearest to him. I say this because of the deep affection expressed in Nabokov's diary entry, but also—considering the writer's opportunistic psychology—because he actually did not make literary use of the sensation of the "creepy, ghostly" movement of those newspapers. That is the very kind of detail he would normally have used to maximum effect. That he resisted likely temptation and didn't make use of the moment points to a higher allegiance.

Then, on the matter of his first poem—the dramatic inspiration he presents in the memoir—Boyd again sets the record straight. He writes:

> In his autobiography he presents the poem as a bolt from the blue, sudden and unprecedented, when in fact for five years or so he had been composing verses in three different languages. The poem he evokes was written not in 1914, but in May 1917, hundreds of poems later:
>
> > The rain has flown and burnt up in flight.
> > I tread the red sand of a path.

Downward a leaf inclines its tip
And drops from its tip a pearl.

Here is some business to ponder. We can, of course, propose what might be called the "sliding scale" of truth—the letter and the spirit—and question how much such discrepancy matters. If we grant, as we are asked to do, that this is the voice of memory we hear, don't we automatically grant an exemption from strict truth?

This might be partially valid retort in theory, but I think there's is no way we can attribute Nabokov's recounting to some hazy forgetfulness, especially as the rest of his presentation relies on the most precise renderings of recollected detail. I would propose, rather, that Nabokov knew the real story and knew how far he was stretching the facts in order to get the effect he was after.

There are those who would protest such leniency, saying something along the lines of, "If I can't trust this scene to be true to what happened, I can't really trust anything." And they would have a point. Such a central part of memoir as a genre is the presentation of self and circumstance as remembered. Indeed, we read the writer's self *through* that presentation. But if we find out that some things, maybe many, have been modified—beyond permissible leeway in shaping—then we no longer have purchase on the teller. We have to wonder what has been altered and why. We may even go so far as to deem the memoirist a maker of fictions, a deceiver.

Finally, though, I find I am not greatly bothered by these discrepancies and want to understand why I'm not. Truth matters. Certainly I'm outraged when I hear about politicians playing fast and loose with the facts. What might make the case of the memoirist different? Speaking for myself, I would say that a memoir like this, a lyric memoir, is not in strict service of the factual, but rather to the re-creation of the self in time. That reaction needs to be responsive to the gist of the main events, even as it offers the interpretation of those events by the way they are depicted.

I've gradually come to understand that even as Nabokov gives us an unprecedented immersion in the most particular details, his overall narrative also fulfills an archetype. Looking back, ignoring the call of the irresistible specifics, the memoir resolves into simple stages. It offers a picture of an idyll cut short, a privileged childhood lost and henceforth mourned, and then a redemption, the deep mourning transformed into art. This bigger story is compelling. And if I think of *Speak, Memory* in this way, I don't have the impulse to begrudge various points of accuracy. Rather, I see Nabokov fashioning his experience into a kind of emblem, using stylistic artifice when needed and working to bring back the spirit of the life he led when younger. All of this as his memory reports on its own authority.

Acknowledgments

To my loyal literary counselors and sounding boards: Chris Benfey, Tom Frick, Bill Pierce and Asked Melnyczuk.

And special gratitude to my daughter Mara, who read these pages with great care and always knew when to say "Dad...you can't say that—you sound like some _____."

To Alden Jones who suggested, and to Robert Lasner who was immediately supportive of the proposal and the pages that followed.